STARTING WELL

Building a Strong Foundation
For a Lifetime of Ministry

By Richard Clinton and Paul Leavenworth

Barnabas Publishers
P.O. Box 6006
Altadena, CA 91003-6006

Printed in the United States of America

Cover Design and Page Layout by D.M. Battermann

ISBN 0974181838

Table of Contents

Preface

Our Vision

This is a book for emerging leaders. Leaders are individuals who have the ability and feel called to influence others to accomplish God's purposes. The essence of leadership in the kingdom of God is influence...not position. You don't have to be a full time worker in Christian ministry to be a leader. God is calling out a people who are willing to serve Him in faithfulness and obedience. This book is targeted for those who are responding to the call of the Master.

Richard and I first met while Richard was a student at Westmont College where I was an administrator. We were later reunited as pastors on the same church staff. During this time of co-labor we discovered that we shared a common burden for the equipping of emerging leaders for the next generation of the church.

Much of the material for this project comes from information and insights that Richard and I have gained from our relationship with Bobby Clinton. Through reading his materials, discussion, and sharing in ministry situations we have been greatly impacted personally and in our ministries.

This project is the result of several years of ministry, dialogue, and experimentation together and individually in the area of Christian growth and leadership development. It is our prayer and hope that the material we share in this book will help challenge and motivate a generation of emerging leaders to trust

God for a greater day for the church.

Our vision is to see this next generation of Christians lay ahold of the resources that Christ won for them through his finished work on the cross and fulfill the great commission in their generation. We trust that this book will in some way contribute to this.

We have co-authored this book because we believe that each of us brings a distinct and important perspective to this material. Richard has unique insights into this material because he has worked so closely with Bobby at Fuller and presented this material to such a variety of people. I have unique insights into this material because I have taught this material while training emerging leaders in church, mission, and college settings.

Each of us have authored separate sections and chapters of this book based on our interests and experience. We have combined these sections and chapters in an attempt to communicate distinct perspectives and experiences while being united by the same vision and goals. We have also integrated our personal experiences into this material to help make this work personal and practical. When we share our individual experiences and/or opinions we will identify them as our own.

The Goals of the Book

This book is designed to share Biblical principles and practical life lessons that will help the reader in his or her process of Christian growth and maturity. We believe that the only hope for the next generation of Christians is to turn to God and begin to live and lead according to His principles. While these principles are important for each person, we are particularly interested in seeing the emerging leaders of the next generation established in sound Biblical principles.

We believe that there are Biblical principles that if applied will help Christians to start, stay, and finish well in their Christian lives and ministries. To this end, we have designed this book to meet the following goals:

1. **To provide an overview of Biblical principles and concepts that relate to building a strong foundation for a lifetime of ministry.**

Chapters 1 and 2 introduce you to the challenge of starting well, staying and finishing well in the ministry. Chapter 1 focuses on what it means to finish well by looking at the characteristics of those who have finished well in their Christian lives and ministries and the common barriers to finishing well. Chapter 2 focuses on the purposes and plans of God for us as His people; how we hinder and/or cooperate with God in these purposes and plans; and strategies for cooperating with God. It looks at the bigger picture of development.

Chapters 3 to 5 describe the initial emphases involved as a leader begins a lifetime of development. Chapter 3 focuses on gaining perspective about our past and how it relates to our future ministry. Chapter 4 focuses on the importance of integrity and our relationship with God as the foundation of our life and ministry. Chapter 5 focuses on the importance of hearing God's voice, and obeying Him. These qualities, (integrity, hearing and obeying God) are key aspects of God's development plan at the beginning of our ministry.

Chapters 6 to 10 describe some basic lessons and issues which are important during the first 10 years of ministry. Chapter 6 deals with some of the more important challenges that emerge during the first 10 years of ministry. These issues represent challenges that emerging leaders need to overcome if they are going to persevere in the ministry. Chapter 7 deals with discovering and developing your giftedness. Chapter 8 focuses on learning to respond in a Godly way to the situations that occur in our lives and ministries.

Chapter 9 focuses on the importance of mentoring and accountability in spiritual growth and ministry effectiveness. Chapter 10 focuses on the importance of calling, vision, and destiny in motivating us to remain faithful over the long haul.

Chapter 11 focuses on developing some strategies which will help us embrace the lessons that leaders need to learn during the first 10 years of ministry.

2. To have an impact on your heart as well as your mind.

We have written this book to be informative, practical, and motivational. We are after your hearts as well as your heads. We hope that this book will motivate many young Christians to take seriously the high calling of the Biblical pattern for mature growth and effective ministry.

We have chosen to share openly and honestly accounts of our own lives. This includes both the failures and successes. We have experienced God's loving faithfulness, patience, and mercy. We have found God's grace is available in each situation.

We believe that people impact people, that a life honestly shared has the power to motive others to honesty, integrity, and faithfulness regardless of life's circumstances. We trust that our lives will impact yours in such a way that you will seek God and his righteousness. Our special prayer is that God will motivate the next generation to pursue God and His purposes wholeheartedly.

3. To provide opportunities for personal evaluation in regards to these basic principles and concepts.

We have provided a series of questions and exercises at the end of each chapter to allow you an opportunity to evaluate yourself in the light of the Biblical principles that have been shared. We would encourage you to take time to work through these questions and exercises after completing a chapter and before starting the next chapter.

We also encourage you to take time to reflect on the insights you might gain from this book. Allow the Holy Spirit to instruct you as you read through this book. Without reflection, you may gain a few insights but might miss a life-transforming encounter with God as He applies His truth to your life.

May God bless you as you read this book. We trust that you will be encouraged to trust God for great things in the midst of the challenges that you will face as the emerging leaders of the next generation of Christ's church.

Introduction

A Time of Crisis or Opportunity?

The closing days of the 20th Century are days of dramatic change and upheaval. With this dramatic change and upheaval has come a growing awareness by many that our world is in crisis. Many researchers, commentators, and authors have documented the crises of war, famine, pollution, poverty, population, recession, depression, abuse, and the list seems to go on and on. One can not turn on the television or pick up a newspaper without being confronted with the reality of crisis.

This Present Crisis

As Christians we should not be surprised by crisis. The Bible clearly reveals that we live in a fallen creation that is "groaning as in the pains of childbirth up to the present time." (Romans 8:22) Jesus revealed that prior to his second coming the world would be characterized by "wars and rumors of wars.. famines and earthquakes in various places." (Matthew 24:6-7) Crisis is the logical expression of a creation that is no longer centered on its Creator. Crisis is inevitable in a fallen world!

The Apostle Paul in Romans 1 reveals that whenever individuals or societies fail to give God their praise and thanks they will suffer the logical consequences of trying to live life apart from God. This ultimately leads to crisis. He wrote,

> *"For since the creation of the world God's invisible qualities-his eternal power and divine nature-have been clearly seen, being understood from what has been made, so that men are without excuse.*
>
> *For although they knew God, they neither glorified him as God nor gave thanks to him, but their thinking became futile and their foolish hearts were darkened. Although they claimed to be wise, they became fools..."*(Romans 1:20-22)

Notice that this failure to give God glory and be thankful results in futility and foolishness. Romans 1:25 further describes this process as an exchange of truth for a lie which ultimately leads individuals and societies to worship and serve created things rather than the Creator. Man begins to worship himself, material things, pleasure, the environment, etc.

At this point, according to Paul in Romans 1:26, God gives individuals and societies over to their natural lusts. Moral anarchy and degradation are the result (verses 26-32). Moral chaos is the core of crisis, because without moral absolutes there are no adequate resources to effectively respond to relational, societal, international, and/or environmental crisis.

Notice the process of digression in this passage. First, individuals or societies fail to acknowledge God which leads to futility and foolishness; then they begin to worship and serve the creation; and finally God turns them over to the control of their natural lusts which leads to moral anarchy and human degradation. This digression is a general pattern of decline that has been experienced by individuals and societies throughout history.

This passage contains a vivid description of what is happening in contemporary western society and unfortunately it is also a picture of much of the Christian subculture. Several researchers have documented the alarming similarities between the moral values and behavior of the general culture and the Christian subculture in such critical areas as values, family, and life-style. Television news programs have given millions of viewers alarming glimpses of the gross materialism and hypocrisy of some Christian leaders.

This trend has resulted in a "credibility gap" for Christianity. There is a growing characterization of Christians as charlatans and bigots in our increasingly secular and relativistic society. There is outright antagonism on the part of many toward those who would espouse moral absolutes. Pro-life verses pro-choice, separation of state and church, personal rights verses traditional values - these issues and many others are the cutting edge issues in a society that has abandoned a Judeo-Christian value system in favor of relativity and personal fulfillment.

The Personal Dimension of This Present Crisis

At a time when an uncompromising demonstration of the dynamic balance of love and truth of Biblical Christianity is most needed, the church, its leaders, and members seem essentially impotent. The moral and ethical failure of prominent leaders, strife among church leaders and members, burnt out leaders who are too tired to continue to play politics, and the compromise and collapse of organizations are all indicative of our impotence.

At the core of our present crises is an individual crisis. It is easy to blame politicians, parents, leaders, the devil, the weather, or an almost infinite number of other possible sources for our present crisis. But the bottom line is that we as individuals are either contributing to the crisis or part of the solution.

It is interesting to note that the word "crisis" is not used in the Bible. Although the Bible describes many crises and how God and people handle them, the Bible seems to be more interested in the solutions to crises than their description or analysis. Jesus provided a context for understanding crisis when he said, "in this world you will have troubles. But take heart! I have overcome the world." (John 16:33)

Crisis for the Christian is an opportunity to see whether or not Jesus really has overcome the world. Crisis is an opportunity to see the promises of God worked out in our own personal, family, and societal lives. Crisis is an opportunity to trust God for what only he can do. Crisis is an invitation for the Christian to be light in darkness!

A Personal Crisis

A few years ago Richard invited me (Paul) to have breakfast with him and his father (Bobby). I was excited about this meeting because I knew that Richard's father was a professor and a life long student of Christian leadership. Although there was no agenda for this breakfast meeting, I hoped that the conversation over breakfast would help me to gain some insights into the struggles that I was having as a new staff pastor at a large church.

I had entered this new ministry situation with many hopes, but now after only a few months I was confused and discouraged. I felt "in over my head," without the personal resources to do what I felt called to do. Key relationships with other staff pastors were strained. Change was an ever present reality. I did not know what to do!

Many questions were on my mind that morning as Richard and I drove together to our breakfast meeting with Bobby. Some of them included:

Had I made a big mistake in taking this pastoral position?

Why couldn't I cope better with the pressures of my life and ministry?

Why was life and ministry so hard?

What was God doing in all of this? How could I discern his will?

What resources did I need to better meet the demands on my life and ministry?

How could I better get along with my colleagues?

What if I failed?

Over breakfast Bobby asked me how things were going. As I

shared with him about my circumstances and questions, I sensed that he cared and understood. After listening to my story, he smiled and shared with me some insights from the Bible on God's process of developing mature Christians.

He shared that God initiates circumstances in the life of Christians to help them grow toward their God given potential. This growth process has a pattern. This developmental process begins with the cultivation of our relationship with Christ which produces Christ-like character. On this foundation a person begins to discover basic ministry resources and lessons which ultimately lead to a mature understanding and expression of Christ in his/her life and ministry.

Bobby's wisdom and practical understanding of Christian growth and leadership gave me a glimpse of hope that there were answers for my questions and resources for my current circumstances. The light came on and I began to understood God's basic process of growing mature Christians in a way that balanced my own responsibility for growth with God's grace.

Since that breakfast meeting my life has been transformed, literally turned upside-down and inside-out. I discovered that I had placed my primary emphasis for life and ministry on the external instead of the internal. I had placed my primary attention on life-style and ministry rather than on relationship with God and character formation.

Consequently, when faced with the demands of life and ministry, I found myself without the resources needed to cope and be effective. As the pressures increased, my exterior life began to crumble revealing spiritual bankruptcy inside. I needed more than tools and techniques to handle my stress and manage my responsibilities, I needed to be transformed.

My personal crisis can be illustrated by the following parable that a friend shared with me several years ago. At the time I found it amusing, but had no idea of how it related to me.

Memorandum

Date: June 1, 28 A.D.

TO: Jesus, Son of Joseph
    Woodcrafters Carpenter Shop
    Nazareth 25331

FROM: Jordon Management Consultants
    Jerusalem 26544

Thank you for submitting the resumes of the twelve men you have picked for management positions in your new organization. All of them have now taken our battery of tests; and we have not only run the results through our computer, but also arranged personal interviews for each of them with our psychologist and vocational aptitude consultant. The profiles of all tests are included, and you will want to study each of them carefully.

As part of our service and for your guidance, we made some general comments, much as an auditor would include some general statements. This is given as a result of staff consultation and comes without any additional fee.

It is the staff opinion that most of your nominees are lacking in background, education and vocational aptitude for the type of enterprise you are undertaking. They do not have the team concept. We would recommend that you continue your search for persons of experience in managerial ability and proven capability.

Simon Peter is emotionally unstable and given to fits of temper. Andrew has absolutely no qualities of leadership. The two brothers, James and John, the sons of Zebedee, place personal interest above company loyalty. Thomas demonstrates a questioning attitude that would tend to undermine morale. We feel that it is our duty to tell you that Matthew has been black-listed by the greater Jerusalem Better Business Bureau. James, the son of Alpheus, and Thaddaeus definitely have radical leanings, and they both registered a high score on the manic-depressive scale.

One of the candidates, however, shows great potential. He is a man of ability and resourcefulness, meets people well, has a keen business mind and has contacts in high places. He is highly motivated, ambitious and responsible. We recommend Judas Iscariot as your controller and right-hand man. All of the other profiles are self-explanatory.

We wish you every success in your new venture[1].

The pressures of life and ministry will eventually reveal the true nature of the heart. Without a radical transformation of heart, we may look good on the outside, but what is on the inside will eventually be revealed.

Although God has been incredibly faithful in my transformation, I have found myself wishing that I would have known sooner about the importance of relationship with God and character formation as the foundation of the maturing Christian life. This understanding could have saved me from making some poor choices which led to personal and ministry frustrations and ineffectiveness.

My story is not unique. Many Christians today are faced with the same type of crisis. Whether in vocational ministry or as lay people trying to live as Christians in our increasingly secular culture, many are finding the challenges of life and ministry overwhelming. Many are asking the same type of questions that I asked. They too are looking for a source from which they can find the resources to live effective Christian lives in this present crisis... or is it really an opportunity?

Crisis, What Crisis?

This personal crisis of relationship with God and character formation is not new. Each generation has had to wrestle with the challenges of what it means to be a Biblical Christians in a fallen world. Each generation also has had the opportunity of finding the resources of the resurrected Christ who empowers to overcome sin, live righteously, and proclaim the favorable year of the Lord.

Most of us are aware of the crisis in culture and in leadership. Some may be in the midst of personal crisis similar to the one Paul describes above. But awareness and analysis of crisis is only an important starting point. We need to take the next step and begin to come up with some solutions!

Crisis is always a great opportunity for the Christian! The Apostle Peter wrote to Christians in the first century who were faced with the crisis of trying to live Christian lives in a pagan culture. He wrote:

> But you are a chosen people, a royal priesthood, a holy nation, a people belonging to God, that you may declare the praises of him who called you out of darkness into his wonderful light. Once you were not a people, but now you are the people of God; once you had not received mercy, but now you have received mercy.
>
> Dear friends, I urge you as aliens and strangers in the world, to abstain from sinful desires, which war against your soul. Live such good lives among the pagans that, though they accuse you of doing wrong, they may see your good deeds and glorify God on the day he visits us. (I Peter 2:9-12)

As Christians, we are called out of darkness into light. We are to be distinct from the general culture as light is distinct from darkness. There is supposed to be a distinction between Christians and non-Christians! Central to this distinction is the ability to abstain from sinful desires (verse 11). As Christians we somehow have the ability to be distinct, not only in behavior, but at the very core of our being.

Jesus taught that the heart is the core of a person's words and behavior (Matthew 15:19). He even went as far as to say that if we hate someone or lust after someone, it is the same in God's view as if we commit murder or adultery (Matthew 5:21-30).

In other words, abstinence from sinful desires involves the radical transformation of the heart of man. As Christians called to be distinct, we must be changed from the inside out. God, in loving relationship with us, is totally committed to our transformation and we have the privilege of submitting to Him in this process.

If we will submit ourselves to the shaping activity of God, He will transform us and we will live lives that are distinctive in our world today. According to verse 12, even the pagans glorified God because of the "good lives" of the Christians. Distinctively Christian relationship, character, and behavior attract the attention of non-believers!

This Present Opportunity!

The opportunity that these first century Christians had is the same type of opportunity that we have today. God is calling his people back to Himself and His purposes for their lives. We are called to be a distinctive people who proclaim and demonstrate the good news that "he (Jesus) himself bore our sins in his body on the tree, so that we might die to sins and live for righteousness; by his wounds you have been healed." (I Peter 2:24).

This present opportunity will not just happen, it will need to be fought for. We will need to learn how to do God's will God's way. We will need to pay the price! J. Oswald Sanders, in his book *Spiritual Leadership* describes the process of qualifying for God's ultimate purposes in the following way,

> Spiritual leaders are not made by election or appointment, by men or any combination of men, nor by conferences or synods. Only God can make them. Simply holding a position of importance does not constitute one a leader, nor do taking courses in leadership or resolving to become a leader. The only method is that of *qualifying* to be a leader. Religious position can be conferred by bishops and boards, but not spiritual authority, which is the prime essential of Christian leadership. That comes often unsought to those who in earlier life have proved themselves worthy of it by spirituality, discipline, ability, and diligence, men who have heeded the command:"Do you seek great things for yourself? Do not seek them." and instead have sought first

the kingdom of God (and his righteousness).
Spiritual leadership is a thing of the Spirit and is
conferred by God alone. When His searching eye
alights on a man who has qualified, He anoints
him with His Spirit and separates him to his
distinctive ministry..." [2]

In each generation God's people are given the opportunity
to respond to this invitation to be a distinct people used to
demonstrate and proclaim hope and opportunity in the midst of
their generations present crisis. In each generation, God calls
out individuals who will take up the reins of leadership. Who
will be the leaders of the next generation? What will be your
response? Will you be a part of the crisis or part of the solution?

Lord God, hear our prayer. Grant that many in this next
generation will qualify for your anointing that "this gospel of the
kingdom shall be proclaimed to all peoples of all nations; then
the end will come!" (Matthew 24:14) AMEN!

Evaluation and Application

1. List what you believe to be the five dominant values of our
   culture and describe how they affect individuals, fami
   lies, and churches.

2. Look up these values in the Bible and see what the Bible
   has to say about them.

3. Evaluate the affect of these values on your own life and
   life-style.

4. List changes that you need to make after examining your
   life in the context of what the Bible has to say.

5. Develop a plan to make these changes.

---

[1] no source

[2] J.Oswald Sanders, Spiritual Leadership. Chicago: Moody Press, 1989, p.25-26

1

Few Leaders Finish Well

"What do you want to be when you grow up?"

When I (Richard) was a young boy, I loved to answer that question. I was going to be either a professional football, basketball or baseball player depending on what time of year you asked me. As a boy, I tended to be optimistic. Can you tell? I still am somewhat of an optimist by nature although I no longer have aspirations of being a professional athlete. These days I have replaced those dreams with other ones.

I have been involved in full time ministry for the last ten years. I am intrigued by Christian leadership and leaders. I have a burning passion to see Christian leaders finish well. My dreams these days revolve around being a leader who finishes well and helping other leaders finish well. At first sight, this doesn't seem very ambitious. However, over the last five years, I have been engaged in studying leaders and leadership. I have come to recognize that the challenge of finishing well is considerable. *You see, few leaders in Christian ministry finish well!*

Biblical Leaders: How did they finish?

A few years ago, Dr. Bobby Clinton, a professor of leadership at Fuller Theological Seminary did a comparative study of leadership in the Scriptures. He published the results in an article entitled "The Mantle of a Mentor[1]." The results were a little shocking to me.

There are approximately 1000 leaders mentioned by name in the Bible. Most of these leaders are mentioned by name only or sometimes are just mentioned in connection with a role. Some of the leaders receive a bit more attention but not very much information is given about their lives. There are about 100 prominent leaders described in the Scriptures.

There are a number of different kinds of leaders described in the Bible. There are patriarchal, military, civil, formal religious (priests), informal religious leaders (prophets), and charismatic (judges) leaders in the Old Testament. In the New Testament, there are the following major leadership types: Jesus (Messiah), apostles, prophets, evangelists, pastors and teachers.

Of the 100 or so prominent leaders, only 49 have enough information given about them to ascertain how they finished their life and ministry. Dr. Clinton developed some categories to help him analyze how the leaders finished. Here are the categories that he used along with a few examples to illustrate his analysis. Granted, this is analysis is based on his judgment and you may differ in your opinion. Even so, the results of his study are interesting.

Types of Finishes

Cut off early   These leaders were taken out of leadership by assassination, killed in battle, prophetically denounced, or overthrown. Some of this activity was directly attributed to God. Some of these were positive and others were negative.

Abimelech, Samson, Absalom, Ahab, Josiah, John the Baptist, James

Finished Poorly These leaders were going down hill in the latter part of their ministry. This might be reflected in their personal relationship with God or in terms of their competency in ministry.

Gideon, Samson, Eli, Saul, Solomon

Finished So-So   These leaders did fairly well but were limited in their ministries because of sin. They did not complete what God had for them or had some negative ramifications surrounding their lives and ministries even though they personally were walking with God.

David, Jehoshaphat, Hezekiah

Finished Well   These leaders were walking with God at the end of their lives. They contributed to God's purposes at a high level. They fulfilled what God had for them to do.

Abraham, Job, Joseph, Joshua, Caleb, Samuel, Elijah, Jeremiah, Daniel, Jesus, John, Paul, Peter

Dr. Clinton admits that the data is not conclusive but there is one overwhelming conclusion that can't be denied. *In the Bible, few leaders finish well!* Only about 30% of the Biblical leaders finished well. That means that 2 out of 3 did not! This is staggering. What does it mean for today? Is there any correlation between the leaders in the Bible and leaders in Christian ministry today? I believe that there is.

In my opinion, the percentage of leaders who finish well in ministry today would be about the same as the Biblical leaders if not a little worse. There are numerous studies being done today on the stress that ministry places on leaders and their families. More and more studies are being done which track what happens to seminary students after they leave school. In a few years, I expect that the results of these studies will be published. The initial reports that I have been hearing would confirm my suspicion that very few leaders are "surviving" a lifetime of ministry much less finishing well.

Is there anything that we can we do about it? What can we learn from the Biblical leaders that might help us today?

Setting Our Sights on Finishing Well

Forewarned is forearmed!   Recently I was playing golf at a tournament with some college friends. We were playing a course that is rated as one of the most difficult courses in the world. There was potential danger on every single shot. Pete Dye, who designed the course made sure of that. Every time that I stood on a new hole, I had to make a choice about where I wanted to try to hit the ball. I was confronted with difficult choices time after time. One of the things that really helped me was that one of the guys that I was playing with had played the course before. On each hole, he would warn me of the potential trouble and suggest where I should try to hit the ball. His knowledge and perspective of the course helped me avoid some of the most difficult spots on the golf course.

A good golf game requires patience, good analysis, plenty of perspective, and the ability to execute what you have planned. Even then, there are variables that can't be controlled, such as the conditions of the course or the weather. Each time you play golf, you have to be flexible and adjust your mind, emotions, and body according to how you feel and the conditions of the course. I believe that it is the challenge of making these adjustments that attracts so many people to the game of golf. It is a difficult and challenging game but if played well is extremely rewarding.

Christian leadership and ministry is difficult and challenging. If done well, it is extremely rewarding. We, as leaders, need all of the knowledge and perspective that we can get. We need people like my friend in the golf game who can warn us of potential danger and things to avoid as well as give us invaluable resources which will help us become more effective.

The apostle Paul realized the importance of learning from others. He writes in Romans 15: 4, "For everything that was written in the past was written to teach us, so that through endurance and the encouragement of the Scriptures we might have hope."   In 1 Corinthians 10: 6, he is speaking about the events, stories, and people that were written about in the Old Testament and says, "Now these things occurred as examples to keep us from setting our hearts on evil things as they did."

Paul is saying that the Scriptures are to be used as warnings and as a source of encouragement and hope. There is much that the Biblical leaders have to say to us about our own leadership. Some of the leaders are to be a great source of encouragement and hope as they modeled what it meant to live righteous lives before God. Other leaders are to stand as warnings and point out dangers that will tempt and challenge leaders who are trying to obey God. Let's learn all that we can from those leaders whose stories are recorded in the Scriptures.

What is a Good Finish?

One of the first things that we can learn from the leaders who finished well in the Bible is what it means to finish well. The first thing that strikes me when I read about the leaders who finished well in the Bible is that they demonstrate that it is possible to finish well. *A leader with God's help can finish well.* In a world in which Christian leaders are being pressed from every side, we need to know that it is not only possible to make it until the end but that we can finish well.

There are six characteristics that stand out about the leaders who finished well in the Scriptures. Not every leader in the Bible had all six of these characteristics. These characteristics paint a vivid portrait of a leader who is finishing well. In my own life, they have become goals or standards by which I measure my growth and progress in life and ministry.

None of us know with certainty what the future holds for us. Life is so short. Moses exhorts all of us when he writes, "Teach us to number our days aright, that we may gain a heart of wisdom." (Psalm 90:12) When do we begin to get the following characteristics established in our lives? Right now!

6 Characteristics of Those Finishing Well

Characteristic 1: RELATIONSHIP WITH GOD
> The leader maintains a <u>personal vibrant relationship</u> with God right up to the end of his/her life. The relationship with God is measured in terms of intimacy, obedience and faithfulness.

Characteristic 2: A LEARNING POSTURE
> The leader maintains a learning posture and learns from various sources such as life, other people, and literature. The leader is a student of life and is able to learn lessons from life.

Characteristic 3: CHRIST-LIKE CHARACTER
> The leader evidences Christ-likeness in his/her character which is manifested in the fruit of the Spirit. The leader's life is characterized by love, joy, peace, patience, kindness, goodness, faithfulness, gentleness and self-control.

Characteristic 4: MAINTAIN CONVICTIONS AND BELIEFS
> The leader lives life based on his/her convictions and truth that God has revealed to him/her. The promises of God are received by faith and decisions are made on the basis of them.

Characteristic 5: ACCOMPLISH GOD'S PURPOSES
> The leader leaves behind an ultimate contribution or a legacy which is a testimony of his/her God honoring life. There are many different kinds of legacies that are left behind. Many are centered on the way the leader was and how he/she lived his/her life. Other legacies are centered around what the leader accomplished in life and ministry.

Characteristic 6: FULFILLED THEIR SENSE OF DESTINY
> The leader walked in a growing awareness of his/her sense of destiny and saw most of it or all of it fulfilled in his/her lifetime. During his/her lifetime, there was a growing sense on the part of the leader that he/she was moving towards accomplishing the things that God has laid out for him/her. Choices and life decisions were made on the basis of this sense of destiny.

These six characteristics paint a vivid picture of what it means to finish well. Not every leader that we have studied has all six characteristics strongly in place. However, an emerging leader ought to use these characteristics as a yardstick or a guideline for shaping his/her life and ministry.

Six Barriers to Finishing Well

Dr. Clinton in his comparative study of the Biblical leaders compared the leaders who finished well with the leaders who didn't. He looked at the leaders who did not finish well and asked,"Why didn't they finish well?" This led to a list of the most common barriers that keep leaders from finishing well.

There are six common barriers that hinder leaders from finishing well. These six barriers were identified in the Biblical leader's lives first and remain common barriers in ministry today.

6 Barriers to Finishing Well

Barrier 1.   FINANCES. THEIR USE AND ABUSE
Leaders, particularly those who have powerful positions make important decisions about finances. A character trait of greed or a lack of integrity will often lead to the improper control and use of money. Numerous leaders have faced this kind of temptation and failed. Money has caused the downfall of quite a few leaders.

Gideon's golden ephod Judges 8
Ananias And Sapphira Acts 5

Barrier 2.   THE ABUSE OF POWER
Leaders in ministry need to operate in power. There are many different sources of power. There is legitimate power that comes with position. There is coercive power that comes as a result of the threat of force. There is spiritual authority which results in powerful influence over people. Power in and of itself is needed in ministry in order to get things done. However, the abuse of power especially when it manifests itself in taking privileges can become a hindrance to finishing well. God will often strike down leaders who abuse power and take privilege over the people they are leading.

Uzziah's usurping of priestly privilege 2 Chronicles 26

Barrier 3.   PRIDE
Pride which is inappropriate and self-centered can lead to the downfall of a leader. As a leader there is a dynamic tension that must be maintained. We must have a healthy respect for ourselves and yet we must recognize that we have nothing that was not given to us by God. He is the one who really allows us to participate and become effective in ministry. Pride can easily lead to poor decisions and sinful behavior.

David's numbering of the people 1 Chronicles 21
Hezekiah's Mistake with the Babylonians Isaiah 39

Barrier 4.   SEXUAL MISCONDUCT
Illicit sexual relationships have been the cause of major downfalls in leadership from the Biblical era to now. Countless leaders have fallen away from ministry because of sinful activity in this realm. Joseph's response to Potiphar's wife in Genesis 39 ought to serve as a model for responding to this kind of temptation.

David's sin with Bathsheba 2 Samuel 11

Barrier 5.   FAMILY RELATIONSHIPS
Problems between spouses or between parents and children or between siblings can easily destroy a leader's ministry. More than ever before, families that live according to Biblical values are needed. Husbands and wives need to learn to love one another and submit to one another. Parents need to learn to teach their children how to live according to Biblical values. Of growing importance in our day is the issue of being single and being in the ministry. How to meet the needs of the single leader in ministry is a tremendous challenge. Failure to meet these needs often leads to poor decisions and becomes a hindrance to finishing well.

Eli and his sons 1 Samuel 2-4
Solomon and his wives 1 Kings 11

Barrier 6.   PLATEAUING
Leaders who are competent in ministry tend to plateau in their growth. What was their very strength (competency in ministry) becomes a weakness. It is possible to minister at a level of competency without the presence of the Holy Spirit. In other words, they have developed ministry skills that can be performed well but without the active presence of God. Plateauing in growth will hinder a leader from finishing well because he/she will not fulfill all that God has for him/her to accomplish.

David in the latter part of his reign just before Absalom's revolt 2 Samuel 15-18

These are not the only barriers that will hinder a leader from finishing well but they are certainly the most common ones. They were prevalent in the Biblical era and continue to hinder leaders today. Proverbs 22:3 say this: "Sensible people will see trouble coming and avoid it, but an unthinking person will walk right into it and regret it later."

We as emerging leaders need to look ahead and see these potential barriers and take steps not to walk right into them. We need to avoid being entrapped by them. When I teach this material in seminars, I often ask the students to realistically evaluate themselves in the light of these six barriers. I ask them, "If one of these barriers were going to hinder you from finishing well, which barrier is most likely?" Most leaders can identify at least 2 barriers that they recognize are key issues for them. I then encourage them to take steps to strengthen themselves in those areas. How would you answer that question?

5 Enhancements Towards Finishing Well

There are no guarantees that any of us will finish well. There is no formula that can be applied in order to ensure success in ministry. However, there are a number of things that we can do in order to enhance our chances of finishing well. It is these enhancements that give me hope and encouragement as I face the challenge of leadership and finishing well.

Enhancement 1. PERSPECTIVE

We need to have a lifetime perspective on ministry. We need to have an overall understanding of what is involved in leadership development over a lifetime. We gain that perspective by studying other leader's lives who have gone before us and learning from them. Hebrews 13: 7-8 exhorts us to do this.   Having perspective on what is happening will greatly enhance a leaders chances of finishing well. He/she will not be completely surprised by the way that God shapes him/her. We need to be able to quickly recognize what God is doing in our lives so that we might respond appropriately. Dr. Clinton has published two books that articulate what he has learned about leadership development[2]. These two sources will greatly help a leader gain some perspective on leadership development.

Enhancement 2. TIMES OF RENEWAL

From time to time, leaders need to experience touches of renewal in their relationship with God. Renewal can come in a number of different ways. There are special moments of intimacy with God or times when God challenges the leader in a special way. Renewal could come through the releasing of a new vision for ministry or through an experience in which God gives the leader a sense of affirmation.

These types of experiences will be needed from time to time. Every leader should expectantly look for these kinds of things to be happening in his/her life or ministry. There are times that God initiates renewal and touches the life of the leader. There are other times when the leader (usually through an extended time of practicing spiritual disciplines) can initiate an experience in which God meets the leader and renewal is the result.

Most leaders who have been effective over a lifetime recognized their need and welcomed renewal experiences.   In western cultures, sociologists and psychologists have studied the developmental cycles of adults and have identified several different key times in which a person needs a touch of renewal. For most adults, somewhere in the mid-thirty's to mid-forties people tend to go through a critical period of transition. During this critical time discipline tends to slack off and there is a tendency to plateau. The person relies on his/her past experiences and skills to get them by. There is frequently a time of confusion about identity and purpose and the need for new vision. An unusual renewal experience with God often helps the leader overcome these tendencies and redirects the leader.

As leaders, we need to be open to these renewal experiences. We must be willing to take steps to receive them when they come. We need to keep in mind that these types of experiences are vital factors in our finishing well.

Enhancement 3. SPIRITUAL DISCIPLINES

Leaders need discipline in many different areas of life and ministry. This is especially true in the area of spiritual disciplines. Over the past 15 years, there has been a strong surge of interest in spiritual disciplines among the Protestant church. The growing desire for intimacy with God coupled with the increasing rate of failure on the part of leaders has created this strong interest. The spiritual disciplines are one of the mediating means for growing in intimacy with God. Authors such as Eugene Peterson, Dallas Willard and Richard Foster are leading the way for Protestants who want to explore and experience the spiritual disciplines. Effectiveness at practicing the spiritual disciplines is one of the primary enhancements toward finishing well. Practicing the spiritual disciplines will enable leaders to focus on Godly priorities and will help the leader eliminate behaviors and attitudes that could lead to his/her downfall.

The apostle Paul exhorted the members of the Corinthian church (and all of his readers) that disciplining himself was a means of inspiring perseverance in the ministry. Paul was around 50 years of age when he wrote the letter and revealed one of the keys to his effectiveness in ministry. He had been in ministry for approximately 20 years when he wrote: "I am serious about finishing well in my Christian ministry. I discipline myself for fear that after challenging others into the Christian life I myself might become a casualty." (1 Corinthians 9:24-27)

Paul believed in practicing discipline. The lack of physical discipline is often an indicator of laxity in the spiritual life as well. Toward the end of his life, Paul encourages Timothy to keep himself fit.

"...take time and trouble to keep yourself spiritually fit. Bodily fitness has a limited value, but spiritual fitness is of unlimited value for it holds promise both for the present life and for the life to come." (2 Timothy 4:7b,8)

Leaders from time to time should assess their state of discipline. In addition to the standard disciplines related to the study of the Word and prayer, I would suggest that you check yourself in the area of other disciplines as well. Richard Foster has written a book that is very helpful in this regard called *Celebration of Discipline*. Dallas Willard's book, *The Spirit of the Disciplines* is also very helpful. Regularly practicing the spiritual disciplines will work to form habits into your life that will greatly enhance your chances of finishing well.

Enhancement 4. LEARNING POSTURE

The single most important antidote to plateauing is to have a well developed learning posture. If a leader is continually learning from a multitude of sources, God has many opportunities to release new energy, vision, and ideas that will greatly help the leader continue in his/her development. Leaders need to develop attitudes and skills concerning learning. Life is a great teacher. Different kinds of experiences can teach many things. Learning from failure as well as success is important.

In western culture, maintaining a learning posture usually involves reading. There are countless materials being published all the time on almost every topic imaginable. Leaders need to acquire skills that allow them to read selectively and yet broadly at the same time. One of the keys that I have discovered to maintaining a learning posture is being accountable to someone for what you are reading and learning.

Besides reading material, there are countless non-formal training events that are available to leaders. Workshops, seminars, and conferences are available from a multitude of ministries that are designed to help leaders in ministry. As leaders, we need to take advantage of the opportunities that are available to us. A good learning posture is like an insurance policy against plateauing. It also forces us to continue to grow and develop. We need to guard ourselves against becoming inflexible leaders as it relates to learning new things. If we become inflexible, we will certainly plateau.

Enhancement 5. MENTORING

Mentoring is a relational process in which one person (the mentor) empowers another person (the mentoree) by sharing God-given resources (timely advice, wisdom, information, emotional support, protection, resources, opportunity) with him/her. If you read Christian biographies of leaders who have finished well, you will discover that on the average, each leader had between 10 to 15 key mentors over their lifetime.

People in other fields such as the military, politics, education, medical have long recognized the importance of the mentoring process. It has only been in recent years that the Christian leaders have begun to realize the importance and value of effective mentoring.

There are many different kinds of mentors and mentoring functions that a leader needs in his/her development process. Disciplers, spiritual guides, counselors, coaches, teachers, sponsors, contemporary and historical models are the types of mentors that we have identified in our studies. Mentors provide two ingredients that are crucial for developing leaders who are serious about finishing well: relationship and accountability. In our day and age, these two ingredients are sorely missing from most leadership training environments.

Simply put, if you are serious about finishing well, you need to find mentors who can hold you accountable in every area of your life and ministry and who will help you avoid the pitfalls that will arise as you move through life. An effective mentor will ensure that you continue to grow and develop.

A Final Challenge

I have some good news and some bad news. Here's the bad news. As I have stated, there is no guarantee in leadership and ministry that you will finish well. And...leadership and ministry is tough and demanding. Finishing well in Christian ministry will require everything that you've got. The reality is that few leaders finish well.

But here's the good news. You won't have to figure it out all by yourself. *God will be with you always!* He will walk with you every step of the way. He will guide you if you will listen. He will teach you if you will learn. He will correct you if you begin to falter. He will empower you and meet your needs when you call out to Him...if you are patient. HE WANTS YOU TO FINISH WELL!

The 5 enhancements that I have outlined are certain to be of great help to you if you are serious about finishing well. They will help you grow in your relationship with God and will give you perspective and encouragement along the way.

Also, I believe that simply knowing that few leaders finish well gives you an advantage. Most leaders are not even aware of the dangers that lie ahead in ministry and leadership. Most leaders just don't take the time to think about finishing well. Most leaders are overwhelmed by the immediate challenges of ministry. Survival is the primary concern of most leaders!

However, if we can start our ministries with an understanding of what finishing well means, we can take steps to ensure that we will keep moving towards a good finish. If we are aware of the potential danger areas, we can make choices from the beginning that will help us avoid them. That is what this book is all about. We are trying to give you a little perspective and help so that you can finish well. *Finishing well begins with starting well.* We are trying to help you by giving you some perspective on the kinds of issues that you will face as you begin to minister to others. Our prayer is that you will start well by learning important lessons and making good choices from the beginning. God wants you to grow and develop into a mature leader. Forewarned is forearmed!

I remember when I was a young child, our family attended a small church in Ohio. I remember that when I was in the sixth grade the pastor preached a year long series on the book of Revelation. Needless to say, I was pretty frightened by the imagery and descriptions that I heard. I remember the pastor urging everyone to make a firm commitment to God. I remember thinking that I was too young to be that serious. I decided to put off making some kind of decision until I was a little older. As a sixth grader, I remember thinking that there were a lot of things out there that I wanted to explore. Three years later, (after a brief period of rebellion and searching), I realized the folly of my thinking and made a serious commitment to Christ.

Many young leaders who are just starting off in the ministry respond in a similar way to the challenge of finishing well. They decide to put off thinking about it until later. They are not going to worry about it. Life is tough enough without worrying about how we are going to finish. There is plenty of time later to think about and plan how I am going to finish. I'm still young and I don't need to concern myself with how I am going to finish. Right? Wrong!

Psychologists tell us that in our older age we don't change much, we simply become more of who we really are. *Young leaders, now is the time to begin thinking about finishing well.* The kinds of attitudes and behaviors that you establish early in life and ministry will control how you will be during the end of ministry. It is far easier to make changes and corrections if they are needed early in the process rather than later. Make choices and decisions now that will help you move towards a good finish.

Richard, what do you want to be when you grow up?

I want to be a Christian leader who has a personal vibrant relationship with God. A leader who continues to learn throughout my whole life. A leader who has Christ-like character and lives according to the Biblical convictions and promises from God. A leader that accomplishes God's destiny and purposes for my life which will involve leaving behind a lasting legacy that testifies to the goodness of God. I want to be a leader who finishes well!

What do you want to be when you grow up?

Evaluation and Application

1. Spend some time reflecting on the end of your life. What do you want to be remembered for? Here is an exercise you can use: Imagine that you are attending your own funeral. What would you want to be said about you? What would you want to be remembered for? What would you want to be written on your tombstone?

2. Take time to study the Biblical leaders. How would you rate their finish? Spend some time reflecting on their stories. What lessons can we learn from them?

3. Look at the admonition in Proverbs 22:3. Answer the question: if one of these barriers were going to hinder you from finishing well, which barrier is the most likely one? Share your answer with a friend. Get some accountability in avoiding the potential trap.

---

[1]There are a number of articles containing the material on finishing well. For a catalog of the articles, contact Barnabas Publishers 2175 N. Holliston Ave. Altadena, Ca 91001.

[2]One book is called The Making of a Leader and is published by NavPress. The other book is a lenghtier treatment of the mase theory and is called Leadership Emergance Theory and is available through Barabas Publishers.

2

Knowing Where You Are Going

As a new Christian in the early 1970's, I (Paul) knew that something dramatic and life changing had happened to me; but I was not sure what it was, or what it meant, or what would happen to me in the future. All I knew was that one day I was headed in one direction and the next day I was headed in another completely different direction.

Although I had grown up in a Christian family, had attended church regularly, and had even gone to yearly summer camps; during my teenage years in the 1960's I had quietly (and later more noisily) rebelled from the faith of my parents. Christianity seemed like a lot of crazy rules and I wanted my freedom and independence.

My search for freedom and independence ultimately led to emptiness and despair as I looked to the "truths" of the youth culture of the 1960's for satisfaction. When I finally gave my life to Christ in 1971, I knew I was a sinner. The prospect of forgiveness and newness of life was really good news to me.

But once I got saved, what then? Some told me to go to church, read the Bible, and pray each day. Others told me to witness. Still others told me to read this book or go to that seminar. Being impressionable, I tried them all and after a brief flurry of activity, I found myself tired, somewhat confused, and unsatisfied. Was this what Christianity was all about?

I was not interested in going back where I came from, but I was not satisfied where I was. What was I to do? Unfortunately it took me several years to begin to understand that doing the right things was not the core of Biblical Christianity. During a premature mid-life crisis in my mid-thirties I began to get a glimpse of the centrality of Biblical Christianity as right relationship with God. At this point in my life I then began to understand that out of a right relationship with God comes transformed character and obedient actions.

How could I have missed this? I had read the Bible, been a regular church attendee, and even gone to seminary. For years I had been trying to live a life pleasing to God instead of enjoying relationship with him. I had been like the little boy who tries to get his busy father's attention by performing some heroic feat. All along I had his attention and acceptance. What God wanted was me!

God's Plan For our Lives

The Bible is very clear about God's plan for our lives. His intention is that once we are saved by Christ's finished work on the cross, we are to become Christlike in relationship with God. This relationship with God is reflected in our character and in our behavior.

The process of becoming Christlike is called sanctification. Sanctification means "to be set apart" unto God for his purposes. The word sanctify in the New Testament has the same root as the words holy and saint. In the Bible sanctification involves being set apart in at least two ways: positionally and progressively.

We are sanctified at conversion (see I Corinthians 6:11). This is positional sanctification. Charles Ryrie in his book So Great Salvation states that "positional sanctification is an actual position that is not dependent on the state of one's spiritual growth and maturity. The one-time offering of our Lord Jesus has sanctified us and perfected us in perpetuity-forever (Hebrews 10:10,14).[1]"

If this is true, why do not all Christians demonstrate this in their daily lives? One answer is that sanctification is progressive or practical as well as positional. Although we are sanctified, we are also becoming sanctified through our obedience day by day. *Our choices affect the reality of our position.*

An illustration might be helpful here. You are poor, struggling to make ends meet. One day you get a phone call from a big city lawyer telling you that your uncle Fred has died and left you an inheritance of several million dollars. All you have to do to collect on the inheritance is to provide proof of your identity and sign some papers and the millions are yours. You are now positionally rich, but practically you are still poor until you follow through on the conditions for actually getting your hands on what is now yours.

This is the condition of many Christians today. We are joint heirs with Christ (Romans 8:17) but we fail to enjoy the benefits of our inheritance because we are not willing to do our part. John Stott in his book *Basic Christianity* states that "clearly we are to do something. Christianity is no mere passive acquiescence in a series of propositions, however true. We may believe in the deity and the salvation of Christ, and acknowledge ourselves to be sinners in need of salvation; but this does not make us Christians. We have to make a personal response to Jesus Christ, committing ourselves unreservedly to Him as our Savior and Lord."[2]

God's plan for our sanctification involves becoming Christlike in relationship with God, in our character, and in our behavior. Jesus had such a close relationship with God that he could say "...that I love the Father and that I do exactly what my Father has commanded me." (John 14:31) Right after saying this He told his disciples that relationship with Him was the basis of fruitfulness in life and ministry. He told them, "I am the vine; you are the branches. If a man remains in me and I in him, he will bear much fruit; apart from me you can do nothing." (John 15:5)

His plan is that out of relationship with Him we will be changed into His likeness and will accomplish His purposes (see Romans 8:28-29, Ephesians 4:11-13, and Philippians 3:10-11). Prior to his crucifixion Jesus prayed for his disciples. He prayed, "Sanctify them by the truth; your word is truth. As you sent me into the world, I have sent them into the world." (John 17:17-18)

After his resurrection he commissioned his disciples saying, "... go and make disciples of all nations..." (Matthew 28: 19, also see Mark 16:15, Luke 24:46-47, John 30:21-23, and Acts 1:8)

It is interesting to note that Jesus had shared with his disciples prior to his commissioning that, "... this gospel of the kingdom will be preached in the whole world as a testimony to all nations, and then the end will come." (Matthew 24:14) It is apparent from this passage that the commission that he gave his disciples must be completed before the end shall come. It is also apparent that the commission that he gave to the first disciples is also our commission as his disciples today.

Again, God's plan is to "set us apart" unto Him for His purposes. Out of relationship with Him, we will become more like Jesus and do what Jesus did. God's plan is for us to "know him and make him known." Now that we know God's plan, let us take a look at this process for fulfilling his plan as it relates to leadership development.

God's Process For Fulfilling His Plan

Over the past dozen years Bobby Clinton, with the help of his students at Fuller Theological Seminary has compiled studies of over 500 Biblical, historical, and contemporary Christian leader's lives. Through these studies a process of Christian and leadership growth has been discovered (see J. Robert Clinton, *The Making of a Leader*, 1988, NavPress).

This process involves six stages (see Figure 2-1 General Time Line) that build on one another as the Christian grows and matures towards fulfillment of God's ultimate purpose for their life. Each stage is unique in its focus and forms the basis for advancement and effectiveness in the next stage. Each stage involves processing unique God ordained circumstances in ways that lead to growth of character, maturity, and expansion of ministry.

Figure 2-1: General Time Line

Phase 1	Phase 2	Phase 3	Phase 4	Phase 5	Phase 6
Sovereign Foundation	Inner-lif Growth	Ministry Maturing	Life Maturing	Convergence	After Glow

We can either cooperate with God in these circumstances which lead to growth in character, maturity, and/or effectiveness; or we can resist God and stagnate in our growth and development as leaders. Three basic elements are involved in the process.

1. God initiates development throughout a lifetime so that we will become more Christlike.

2. We can respond positively or negatively to God's sovereign initiation in our life.

3. If we respond positively, we grow in Christlike character, maturity, and effectiveness; but if we respond negatively, we will stagnate until we respond positively to that issue.

These three elements form the basis for our growth, maturity ,and effectiveness as we progress from stage to stage in our development as Christians.

As we have seen in the last chapter, not every leader finishes well. There is no guarantee that we will progress in our leadership development through all six stages. But it is God's intention that each one of us develop into complete maturity. He has given us His Son, His word, His Spirit, the church, as well as a host of Biblical, historical, and contemporary examples to learn from. He want us to learn to appropriate all that He has done for us and given us so that we might "run with perseverance the race marked out for us" (see Hebrews 12:1-3).

Developmental Stages For Life and Leadership

Stage 1 - Sovereign Foundations

The first stage is called "sovereign foundations." This stage involves God sovereignly laying a foundation for a person's life through his/her family, his/her social and historical context. God places each of us in a relational and historical context that will maximize our opportunities to know Him and to become the person whom He desires us to become.

This view of God's sovereign involvement in the foundational aspects of our birth, race, family, culture, and historical context is described in Psalms 139:13-16,

> *"For you created my inmost being;*
> *You knit me together in my mother's womb.*
> *I praise you because I am fearfully and wonderfully made;*
> *Your works are wonderful, I know that full well.*
> *My frame was not hidden from you*
>   *when I was made in the secret place.*
> *When I was woven together in the depths of the earth,*
> *Your eyes saw my unformed body.*
> *All the days ordained for me were written in your book*
>   *before one of them came to be."*

God knows us! He knows everything about us. And He knows of our sinfulness and what it will take to bring us to Him. He allows us to be exposed to the devastating consequences of sin in relationships, in society, and in our world so that we will recognize our need for Him. Paul in Romans 3 describes the nature of sinful humanity when he writes,

> *There is no one righteous, not even one;*
> *There is no one who understands, no one who seeks God.*
> *All have turned away, they have together become worthless;*
> *There is no one who does good, not even one.*

Their throats are open graves; their tongues practice deceit.
The poison viper is on their lips.
Their mouths are full of cursing and bitterness.
Their feet are swift to shed blood; ruin and misery mark
their ways, and the way of peace they do not know.
There is no fear of God before their eyes. (verses 11-18)

He also gives us ample opportunities to know him. Even in cultures where the gospel has not yet been proclaimed, God has given a witness in creation and conscience (Romans 1:20). But in cultures such as ours, He has also given us the Scriptures and the witness of the church. If those who have not been exposed to the gospel are without excuse, how much more are we responsible to God for his witness to us?

Not only does God know what it will take to bring us to him, He loves us (see John 3:16) and knows of our potential to love Him and become all that He has destined us to be. Each of us has a destiny to have a love relationship with God and to fulfill a specially designed role in God's plan to save a lost humanity from their sin.

The reality of God's sovereignty in these foundational matters is not meant to diminish the tragedy and heartache of broken relationships or human inhumanity. God does not allow any circumstances to take place in our lives that He has not faced on our behalf (see Hebrews 4:15-16) and that He can not use for good (see Romans 8:28). Human heartache and tragedy can become the context for growth and blessing.

In Chapter 3, we will be looking at the issue of the sovereignty of God as it relates to our foundations. In that chapter, we will address the issue of how God works in our lives during this foundational time even if we don't know Him or are not following Him. The sovereign foundations development phase is all about God establishing us in our context of relationships, our personality, our situational context and the initial establishment of our relationship with Him.

Stage 2 - Inner-Life Growth

The second stage is called "inner-life growth." This stage involves developing a foundational relationship with God out of which Christlike character and maturity develop. During inner-life growth we make our initial commitment to Christ as Savior and Lord and begin to learn to relate to Him In this process, He begins to transform us. We incorporate the basic disciplines of the faith into our relationship while learning how to obediently respond to specific checks that God initiates for character development and growth (see Figure 2-2 - Characteristics of Inner-Life Growth Stage).

Figure 2-2 - Characteristics of Inner-Life Growth Stage

Disciplines	Checks
Inward Disciplines	Integrity Checks
Outward Disciplines	Obedience Checks
Corporate Disciplines	Word Checks

The development of a devotional life (not a just a "time") is critical during this stage. We want to spend time with this person who loves us so much that He gave his life that we might be set free from the bondage of our sin. Love is a powerful reality. If you have ever been in love, been around some one in love, or wished you were in love; you know that people in love want to spend time with each other, do things with each other, and do things for each other. When we receive a letter or phone call from our loved one, we drop everything in order to hear what they have to say. When our behavior is displeasing to our loved one, we try to change it. This is the reality of our new relationship with Christ, our loved one.

A devotional life based on a love relationship with God is vital for subsequent growth and effectiveness in one's Christian life. From our relationship with God we derive the resources necessary to obediently face life's challenges.

This type of devotional life has historically been characterized by "the disciplines" of the faith. These include inward, outward, and corporate disciplines (see Richard J. Foster, *The Celebration of Discipline,* 1988, Harper & Row). The inward disciplines include study, meditation, prayer, and fasting. The outward disciplines include simplicity, solitude, submission, and service. The corporate disciplines include confession, guidance, worship, and celebration.

These disciplines of the faith are expressions of love and avenues of grace. They are not works or merit. We do not gain approval or promotion through the disciplines. We gain access to a growing and maturing relationship with God. Through the disciplines we get to know God, ourselves, and others. We learn how to commune with God, be transformed, and to forgive and serve. God becomes the wellspring of life abundant (see John 4:13-14, 10:10). His commandments are no longer burdensome (see I John 5:3).

The importance of an intimate relationship with God based in the spiritual disciplines of the faith is well documented in Biblical, historical, and contemporary leaders who have started, stayed, and finished well (see F. B. Meyer's "Classic Portraits" series published by Christian Literature Crusade or V. Raymond Edman's book *They Found the Secret,* 1984, Zondervan). They are critical!

Out of our growing relationship with God will come God initiated opportunities for the transformation of our character from self-centeredness to Christ-likeness. God initiates this process in the inner-life growth stage in three primary areas. These areas include integrity, obedience, and word checks.

Integrity checks are special tests that God initiates to reveal the true intentions of our heart and when passed serve as a springboard for the expansion of a person's capacity to be trusted by God. Obedience checks are special tests that reveal our willingness to obey God regardless of circumstances and apparent consequences and when passed lead to the realization of God's promises. Word checks are special tests that reveal the ability to receive and understand a word from God, and allow God to work out the fulfillment of this word. One can be involved in one, two, or all three of these checks at a time. We will look at these more closely in Chapter 5.

An example of faithfulness in the inner-life growth stage is Daniel. He was part of the exiles taken to Babylon (Daniel 1:3).

From there he was chosen by Nebuchadnezzar king of Babylon to be trained for three years as preparation for government service (Daniel 1:5). During this training time Daniel and three of his friends were asked to eat and drink certain types of food and wines that were in violation to Jewish law (Daniel 1:5). Daniel "resolved not to defile himself with the royal food and wine..." (Daniel 1:8).

This is an example of an integrity and obedience check (and possibly a word check). Daniel knew that to eat and drink the king's food and wine was a violation of God's law. He also knew that to defy the king could result in his punishment and possible death (see chief official's response in verse 10). This was a test of both his integrity and obedience.

Because Daniel resolved not to defile himself, he placed himself in a position for God to intervene on his behalf. Probably in prayer, Daniel came up with the idea of approaching the chief official about an "experimental diet" (Daniel 1:8). This would be an example of a word check. When he approached the chief officer with this idea, God gave him favor and caused the officer to show sympathy (Daniel 1:9).

The officer agreed to the experiment (Daniel 1:14) and Daniel and his three friends prospered in health, knowledge, and understanding (Daniel 1:15-17). At the end of the three years of training they were found to be ten times better in wisdom and understanding than any of the other magicians and enchanters in the whole kingdom (Daniel 1:20).

The inner life growth phase is all about developing relationship with God. In the context of that relationship, God will begin to work on establishing Godly leadership character in our lives. This Godly character will form the basis of our life and effectiveness in ministry even as it did with Daniel.

Stage 3 - Ministry Maturing

The third stage is called "ministry maturing." This stage involves developing and maturing in effective ministry through the identification and application of one's gift mix and ministry skills. This process can take place in either a vocational or lay ministry context where one can be challenged to respond positively to ministry tasks, relationships, conflicts, and authority. It is in this initial phase of ministry involvement that a person begins to discover their giftedness.

A person's giftedness is made up of a combination of spiritual gifts, natural abilities, and acquired skills. It is through the obedient use of your gift mix that you will probably have your most rewarding and influential opportunities in ministry. Ministry skills refer to those specific skills that you acquire in ministry situations that help you to perform ministry tasks more effectively. Examples of this are Biblical counseling skills, church management skills, or teaching skills.

The awareness of gift mix and ministry skills is important but it is in the context of ministry tasks, relationships, conflict, and submission to authority that we learn how to effectively minister. Relationship with God and others is still the priority in this stage (as in all stages). To accomplish a task in an unloving manner is not mature ministry. God's plans must always be accomplished God's way!

Moses is a good example of this. At the age of forty he tried to accomplish God's purpose to deliver Israel through his own efforts (Exodus 2:12). His murder of the Egyptian who was mistreating a Hebrew led to rejection and flight to the backside of Midian (Exodus 2:15). Although he had a sense of God's purpose for his life (see Hebrews 11:24-25) he did not understand God's way. Consequently, his first attempt at accomplishing God's purpose lead to disastrous consequences.

Although we do not know very much about Moses' life for the next forty years, it is very apparent that something dramatic happened to him during those years of building a family and tending sheep (see Acts 7:29-34). When we encounter Moses again after forty years, if anything, he lacked confidence in his abilities (Exodus 3:11). He had learned dependence upon God during this time. Now he was ready to do God's purposes God's way!

This phase of leadership development is centered around developing ministry skills in both relationships and tasks. This involves learning how to get things done through the use of your giftedness.

Stage 4 - Life Maturing

The fourth stage of development is "Life Maturing." This stage involves developing a personal and mature Biblical philosophy of ministry. A personal and mature Biblical philosophy of ministry is foundational for convergence in stage 5 when inner-life preparation, a person's giftedness, ministry experience, and ministry philosophy come together in the effective and fruitful expression of one's destiny or ultimate purpose.

Ministry philosophy refers to the ideas, values, and principles that a Christian uses for decision making, for exercising influence, and for evaluating self, relationships, and ministry effectiveness. Four major lessons must be learned during this stage.

1. Mature ministry flows out of mature character.
2. Mature character is formed through obedience in difficult situations.
3. Many Christians go through difficult situations without knowing of the potential benefits. It is important to discover God in the midst of difficult situations and learn of Him.
4. Mature leaders operate with spiritual authority as their primary base of power. In this development phase, leaders learn how spiritual authority is developed. In essence, spiritual authority is not a goal but a byproduct of obedience. Obedience in the difficult seasons of life create a depth of Godly character that exudes spiritual authority.[3]

The process of developing a personal philosophy of ministry involves three factors and three sub-stages. The first factor is the Biblical dynamic. The basis of any mature ministry philosophy must be the Bible. The second factor is our personal giftedness. We tend to see life and ministry through the grid of our giftedness. And the third factor is our personal experience. We tend to see "reality" from our own experience. Neither our giftedness nor experience should contradict the Biblical dynamic, but they will play a significant role in the development of our ministry philosophy.

Figure 2-4 - Characteristics of Life Maturing Stage

Factors	Sub-Stages
Biblical Dynamics	Osmosis
Personal Gift Mix	Baby Steps
Personal Experience	Maturity

Ministry philosophy develops over time. We have a ministry philosophy in earlier stages but it is not usually personal and/or mature. Ministry philosophy usually develops through the three sub-stages of osmosis, baby steps, and maturity. Osmosis refers to the beginning stages of developing a ministry philosophy when we learn primarily by observation of others and by experimentation. We are attracted to someone's ministry so we try to minister just like that person. We read a book or go to a seminar and try to implement what we learned in our own situation.

The next sub-stage after osmosis is called baby steps. In the baby step sub-stage we learn by intentional design and evaluation. We begin the seek god for Biblical principles for life and leadership and evaluate our performance in this basis. We begin to ask questions about whether traditional or contemporary ways of doing things are necessarily God's ways.

The final sub-stage is maturity. In this stage Christians are able to articulate their own ministry philosophy in terms of lifestyle. Ministry philosophy is no longer theoretical, it is now practical and forms the basis for decision making, exercising influence, and evaluation.

Paul is a good example of the development of a mature ministry philosophy. When Paul was first saved (Acts 9) he was called to be God's "chosen instrument to carry {God's} name to the Gentiles..."(verse 15). Immediately after his conversion, filling with the Holy Spirit, and baptism (verses 17-18) he began to preach in the synagogues (verse 20). His ministry philosophy at this stage was greatly influenced by Jewish customs and what he had seen the early Christians doing (see Acts 6:8 - 8:1). This is an example of the sub-stage of osmosis.

Later Paul would spend time with the Apostles in Jerusalem (Acts 9:26-30, 11:29-30 and Galatians 1:18-19), spend time with Christ in the deserts of Arabia (Galatians 1:15-17), and work and minister in Tarsus (Acts 9:30, 11:25) and Antioch (Acts 9:26 - 13:3). During this time of early ministry Paul must have searched the Scriptures to develop a Biblical ministry philosophy consistent with his calling. This is an example of the sub-stage of baby steps.

Finally Barnabas and Paul, while ministering to the Gentile church at Antioch (Acts 11:26, 13:1), were set aside for pioneer ministry to the Gentiles in Asia Minor (Acts 13:2-3). During this "first missionary journey" Paul further develops his ministry philosophy to include a strategy for evangelism, discipleship, and leadership development. This ministry philosophy would become the basis for his future ministry to the Gentiles.

The Life Maturing development phase is all about a deepening of character and the development of a mature ministry philosophy. A mature ministry philosophy allows a person to operate in ministry with efficiency (which is doing things very well) AND effectiveness (which is doing the right things very well).

Stage 5: Convergence

The fifth stage of development is "convergence." This stage involves the mature coming together of inner-life preparation, ministry maturing, and ministry philosophy to fulfill one's destiny or ultimate purpose. Convergence involves the coming together of five major and six minor factors. The major factors include dependence upon God, giftedness, ministry philosophy, role, and influence. The minor factors include experience, personality, location, opportunity, prophecy, and destiny (see Figure 2-5 - Characteristics of Convergence stage). In convergence, the leader has the sense that things have come together in such a way that he/she is operating at the maximum potential in leadership that God desired for him/her.

Figure 2-5 - Characteristics of Convergence Stage

Major Factors	Minor Factors
Dependence of God	Experience
Giftedness	Personality
Ministry Philosophy	Location
Role -The Right One	Opportunity
Influence - Appropriate level	Prophecy
	Destiny

Joseph is a good example of a leader who reached convergence. As a young man of about seventeen (Genesis 37:2) he received two prophetic dreams about his future destiny as a leader (Genesis 37:5-11). Some thirteen years later (Genesis 41:46) when Joseph was thirty years old these dreams were fulfilled in part when he was promoted to the position of Prime Minister of Egypt (Genesis 41:411-43). But prior to this fulfillment, Joseph had to learn faithfulness to God in the pit (Genesis 37), in Potiphar's house (Genesis 39), and in prison (Genesis 39-41). The ultimate fulfillment of these dreams came seven years after Joseph became Prime Minister when Jacob sent ten of his sons to buy grain (Genesis 42:6-7).

In the life of Joseph we see the coming together of the five major factors of convergence. He had learned dependence upon God in very difficult and painful circumstances; his giftedness in interpreting dreams, serving, and administration had surfaced; his ministry philosophy had been developed in lowly service; God had sovereignly given him his role; and he was able to influence not only the affairs of Egypt but the destiny of Israel.

It is important to note that when reunited with his brothers who had sold him into slavery, his response was "... it was not you who sent me here, but God" (Genesis 45:8). Later he would reflect to his brothers the reality of his life by saying, "you intended to harm me, but God intended it for good to accomplish what is now being done, the saving of many lives." (Genesis 50:20) Joseph, who suffered so much because of his brothers, had been so transformed by his relationship with God that he could see and experience the ultimate good in it all.

It is important to note that very few leaders every reach convergence. In fact, most leaders do not. Many leaders experience what we call "mini-convergence" where 2 or 3 of the factors come together. There are a lot of reasons for this. Some of which are related to the leader himself/herself. Some of which are out of his/her control.

Stage 6 - Afterglow

The final stage is "afterglow." This stage is characterized by the enjoyment and influence available to a person who has completed their life calling or destiny. This stage is rarely attained, but when convergence has been realized and God grants additional years to a Christian they can continue to have a major influence through their relationship with others.

There is no recognizable task associated with this stage. This is a stage in which a Christian is able to enjoy the blessings of a life of obedience. From the status of having finished well comes encouragement and influence for the next generations of Christians.

An example of afterglow is seen in the life of Caleb. This little know saint was characterized by having "a different spirit" that followed God "wholeheartedly" (Numbers 14:24). He was one of the twelve spies selected by Moses to survey the land of Canaan (Numbers 13:6). He, along with Joshua, gave the minority report about Canaan. He said, "if the Lord is pleased with us, he will lead us into that land...and will give it to us" (Numbers 14:8).

Caleb and Joshua were the only men from their generation who were allowed to enter the land. All the rest had died in the wilderness, never experiencing their inheritance in the land. Once in the land Caleb claimed Hebron which God had promised him as his inheritance (see Deuteronomy 1:36) and claimed that, "I am still as strong today as the day Moses sent me out; I am just as vigorous to go out to battle now as I was then." (Joshua 14:11) Caleb was eighty-five when he said this!

Caleb then captured Hebron by defeating the three Anakite giants (Joshua 15:14) and established his home there. He gave his daughter Ascah to Othniel in marriage (Joshua 15:17) and gave the new couple the land of the upper and lower springs (Joshua 15:19). Hebron later became a Levitical town of refuge (Joshua 21:12) and Othniel became the first Judge of Israel (Judges 3:10).

Caleb's destiny was to take Hebron and once he had accomplished that he was able to enjoy its blessings and share them with his family and through Othniel with the whole nation. This is afterglow.

Now that we have a general idea of God's plan and his process for achieving that plan in our individual lives, we can begin to look at specific issues as they relate to sovereign foundations, inner-life growth, and ministry maturing. *In this book, we have chosen to focus on the first 10 years of ministry or so.* These three stages serve as the foundation for starting well in our Christian lives and ministries.

Evaluation and Application

1. Look up the Biblical passages mentioned in the section on God's plan in this chapter.

2. Prayerfully evaluate yourself on the basis of these passages. Are you realizing your inheritance as a Christian to its fullest?

3. If not, why not? Prayerfully ask God to reveal to you what areas of your life/life-style need to be changed in order for you to realize your inheritance.

4. Develop a plan to make these changes.

5. Evaluate these plans periodically.

---

[1] Charles Ryrie, So Great Salvation, Wheaton, IL, 1989, p.151.

[2] John R.W. Stott, Basic Christianity, Downers Grove, IL: Intervarsity Press, 1971, p. 107.

[3] J. Robert Clinton, The Making of a Leader, Colorado Springs, CO: NavPress, 1988, p.155

3

Beginnings:
The Early Formation of a Leader

"Richard, you don't understand," she said in a choked voice with tears running down her face. "You don't know about my past...the things I've done...the kind of family I was raised in. God could never use me in the ways that you are suggesting...."

Have you ever had a conversation like this? Have you ever thought about yourself in this way? If you are normal (and honest), you have. I don't know of very many young people these days who feel "worthy" of serving as one of God's leaders.

We live in a culture in which moral values and good family values are all but gone. Young children today are bombarded by media messages that fill their lives and minds with empty promises and a set of values that evaporate as quickly as the morning dew. The statistics and percentages of young people who come out of broken, wounded families are staggering to say the least. Dysfunctionality is becoming a common description of life and family.

When you begin to add all of these factors together and think about them in the light of Christian leadership development, it can be a little overwhelming. A few years ago, I was the pastor of a young adult ministry in a large Southern California church. One of my tasks in overseeing the group was to train up leaders from the group who would lead various ministries among their peers. As I began the task of identifying and training leaders, I was overwhelmed by the amount of hurt, woundedness and poor self images that the young adults brought to church with them. I found out very quickly that many of them needed to receive healing and gain an understanding of God's grace before I could even talk about leadership and responsibility. The short conversation that I recorded at the beginning of the chapter was repeated on numerous occasions. Slowly but surely, a number of them began to believe that God could overcome their past hurts and sin and could use them in ministry.

In this chapter, I want to address the issue of a leader's early formation. I want to give you some perspective on how to find God's involvement in your past. I want to teach you to trace the sovereign hand of God through the circumstances of your beginnings. I believe that this chapter can be one of the most healing chapters in this book. I would encourage you to open your heart as you read and allow the Spirit of God to touch you and bring healing perspective to you.

God, Where Were You?

In my experience of training and releasing emerging leaders into ministry, I have discovered that some young leaders must deal with very painful issues surrounding a difficult past. In such circumstances, the young leader needs to gain perspective on the past, as he/she attempts to understand where the "loving God" was when he/she was being abused and harmed during their childhood or adolescence. Many of the questions begin with...if God is sovereign and is loving, kind, merciful, then why did this thing or that situation happen to me?

A person's image of God can often be skewed because of these experiences and a lack of understanding. This is especially true when the circumstances are negative and hurtful. More and more emerging Christian leaders come out of broken, hurtful upbringings. Some young leaders are hurt by the effects of their own sin and rebellion. Others are impacted and wounded by circumstances that are beyond their control.

One of the best books that I read during a painful period

in my own past was a book about suffering written by Peter Kreeft called *Making Sense Out of Suffering*. It is an excellent book that is written in a unique style which makes for easy reading. In the book, the author says that God's answer to the issue or problem of suffering is that God came and suffered and that God is with us in our suffering. This sounds like a simple solution to the problem of why God allows suffering but it is profound in its implications. Over the years, I have tried to teach myself to find God in the midst of the suffering. This is the key to understanding God's involvement in your own past and any suffering that you may have experienced.

Is it possible to learn to see God's hand in your past? How can we shed some light on our early formative years so that we can gain God's perspective on them? Is it possible to come from a broken family or a negative situation and still start well in Christian leadership? I believe that it is! *The key is in learning to see your past in light of God's sovereign activity.*

In order to gain this perspective, you need to begin by believing that God is sovereign. A simple definition of God's sovereignty would be that everything is under His control. Nothing happens that God does not either allow to happen or initiates Himself. I don't believe that God is surprised by the events, choices and details of our lives. *Choosing to believe in the sovereignty of God is the first step in gaining His perspective on your past.*

Beyond a basic trust in God and His sovereign purposes, there are three things that I think are helpful in understanding what God was doing in your past. The first has to do with ministry to others. There is a definite pattern that can be observed. Step 1: God takes you through a situation and meets you in it. You learn about God and His ways. Step 2: Because you personally go through the situation, you understand the special needs of a person who is going through a similar situation. You have a special awareness or insight into how God meets a person in that kind of situation. Step 3: You are able to comfort others in similar circumstances and testify to God's faithfulness and love in a credible way because of your own experience. You have a basic trust and faith in God's ability to bring healing because you have received it yourself. Paul comments on this in his second letter to the church in Corinth. He says,

> *"Let us give thanks to the God and Father of our Lord Jesus Christ, the merciful Father, the God from whom all help comes! He helps us in all our troubles, so that we are able to help others who have all kinds of troubles, using the same help that we ourselves have received from God. Just as we have a share in Christ's many sufferings, so also through Christ we share in God's great help."* (2 Corinthians 1:3-5)

When you look at various leaders in ministry, it is easy to see this pattern. God often uses people to reach others who are facing or have faced similar circumstances as their own. Some of you have faced or are facing difficulty in understanding your past. Ask yourself how God met you and how God is continuing to meet you. God may want to use you to reach many others who are in a similar situation.

A second thing that is helpful in understanding your past is to understand the process of how God develops people. Paul touched on this process (sanctification) in the previous chapter. If we have an understanding of how God develops people, we can look back at our past circumstances in the light of God's shaping hand. Everything that happened was part of an overall plan that God sets in motion for each one of us. Ephesians 2:8-10 teaches us that each one of us was saved by grace and that God is "hand-crafting" us and preparing us to accomplish the good works that He set out for us before the beginning of time. I have often been staggered by trying to understand the awesome sovereignty and planning of God. He uses each person, circumstance, and event to shape us and prepare us for accomplishing our part of His eternal redemptive plan.

The third thing that truly helps us understand the events of our lives is the passage of time. With the passage of time, we have a better chance of gaining perspective on the situations we went through. I've heard it said that "Hindsight is 20/20." I believe that this is true for the most part. The trick is getting far enough ahead that it is truly hindsight when you look back. Often, emerging leaders are not far enough ahead to look back on their early formation in hindsight. Sometimes, when you look back the only truthful answer is "I don't know what God was trying to do in that situation." I suspect that there are some questions and circumstances that will not be understood or answered until we look back from heaven.

Biblical Case Studies

There are many different characters in Scripture that demonstrate the sovereign hand of God in preparing leaders for their role in the redemptive drama. I will choose three of my favorites to illustrate the sovereign hand of God. Two of these characters came from negative family backgrounds and the last comes from a positive background. Each of them demonstrates the sovereign hand of God in a graphic way.

Joseph

Joseph is a familiar Biblical character. In Sunday School, many of us learned the stories about how he was the favorite son and got the multi-colored robe from his father. Have you ever thought about the family climate that he was raised in? His father was renowned for his deceitfulness and deviousness. His mother was vying for supremacy and privilege in the household with Leah. There were numerous siblings. Violence, competitiveness, and, deceitfulness were commonplace among the sons of Jacob. Can you imagine being raised in a family like this? It was not a very peaceful environment. On top of this, Joseph's mother died giving birth to Benjamin. Joseph would have had to learn to fend for himself pretty early in life. He became his father's favorite and his brothers began to hate him. On top of this, God gave him dreams concerning his future and how he would rule over his brothers. This increased their hatred.

This is the initial stage of Joseph's preparation for his role in God's redemptive drama. It is hard to believe that this is one of the most significant leaders during this stage of God's redemptive plan. We hear nothing about Joseph's spirituality or relationship to God.

He is sold into slavery at an early age (estimated to be a teen-ager). In Egypt, he demonstrates that he is aware of God and has some kind of relationship with Him during his encounter with Potiphar's wife. He recognized that it would be a sin against God to sleep with her. In prison, Joseph is aware that God is the one who gives the ability to interpret dreams. Joseph may or may not been aware of God's presence being with him and grant-ing him success.

During the famine, Joseph's brothers came down to Egypt to buy grain. At this point, approximately 18 years later Joseph would have remembered the dreams that he had! He had lived as a slave and in prison cut off and isolated from his family. What a temptation it must have been to want to hurt his brothers. Revenge was a highly valued matter of principle in that culture. In my opinion, Joseph wrestled with these temptations as evi-denced by the way he treated his brothers in the early encoun-ters with them.

Somehow in the end, Joseph recognized the sovereign hand of God and responded to God in faith. When he revealed his true identity to his brothers, he says, "Now do not be upset or blame yourselves because you sold me here. It was really God who sent me ahead of you to save people's lives...God sent me ahead of you to rescue you in this amazing way and to make sure that you and your descendants survive." (Genesis 45:5,7)

Joseph and his family wept together and forgave one another as they all recognized the sovereign hand of God. What an in-credible story! I have often wondered how I would have re-sponded if I were in Joseph's situation. Somehow he maintained an openness to God during his life in Egypt. It is possible to come out of an extremely negative family background and be mightily used by God. The key is that Joseph somehow stayed open to God and placed his faith in Him.

Jephthah

Jephthah was one of the deliverers that God raised up dur-ing the time of the judges. To truly understand his story, you need to understand the cyclical nature of this period of time in

Israel's history. The people of Israel were not under any kind of a central unified government. The Bible says that each person did what was right in their own eyes. It was a dark period in the history of Israel.   Here is how the cycle would operate: the people would reject God and worship other gods. God would give them over to these gods and allow them to be defeated in war, ravaged by the surrounding peoples. The people in their misery would recognize their sin and cry out to God in repentance. God would eventually respond by raising up a deliverer who would lead them in victory against their enemies. The deliverer would then act as a judge for the people. The judge would die and the people would turn away from God and repeat the initial stages of the cycle.

To understand Jephthah's story, you need to see the cycle of events in action. Jephthah was the son of a prostitute. He was taken into the father's family as an illegitimate son. However, the other children with the agreement of the community leaders did not want to share any of their inheritance with him so they drove him out of the community.   In those days, if you didn't belong to a community or family, there were not very many job options available. In order to escape with his life, he fled to the land of Tob.

He evidently was perceived to be a strong leader because he attracted a group of followers. The Bible describes these followers as worthless men. They lived off the land by marauding and pillaging.   Does this sound like great preparation and training for being a deliverer of Israel?   From God's perspective, it was. You see, the Ammonites had been dominating the land for nearly 18 years.   During this time, God was preparing a deliverer...Jephthah.

What kinds of things do you think Jephthah learned during his preparation and training?   I think he learned things about warfare tactics, crisis leadership, how to deal with devious followers, negotiating skills and somehow, he learned that the Lord of Israel is the one who gives the victory.

Guess what kind of leader God needed to deliver the people from the Ammonites?   Exactly, during the entire time that the Ammonites were oppressing and persecuting the Israelites in

Gilead, God was preparing His deliverer in the land of Tob. Can you see the sovereign hand of God? He was moving, shaping and preparing Jephthah for leadership in Israel.

I find it interesting that Jephthah is one of the few leaders that is mentioned by name in the hall of faith in Hebrews 11. He is remembered in Scripture as being a leader who operated in faith.

Barnabas

The character of Barnabas in the pages of the book of Acts plays a critical role. What do we know about Barnabas' upbringing or background? In Acts 4:36 we are told that Joseph (Barnabas) was a Levite was born in Cyprus. He was apparently wealthy enough to own some property which he sold and brought the money to the apostles. This verse says a lot about Barnabas. The apostles called him Barnabas because it means "one who encourages". How do you get to be a person like this? If psychologists are correct in their theories, much of this attitude would have been learned early in his life. We can't know for sure but maybe his father or mother helped to ingrain these kind of attitudes.

It is also significant that he was born and raised in Cyprus. Cyprus was an island community that had a significant trading port. He would certainly have been bi-cultural and probably spoke several different languages.

Another value that would have been ingrained at an early stage in life would have been his willingness to be generous. His sale of the property and gift to the church stands in stark contrast with Ananias and Sapphira whose story comes immediately after his.

These three key insights into the person and character of Barnabas play a crucial role throughout the book of Acts and in the history of Christendom. No one else but Barnabas would associate with Saul the persecutor of the church. Barnabas, the encourager listens to his story and believes in Saul enough to link him to the apostles in Jerusalem. Barnabas risked his credibility in order to sponsor Saul. Without Barnabas, there would not have been a Paul in the early church. He eventually linked him into the mainstream through his work in the church at Antioch.

Secondly, when Christianity began to be spread to the gentiles, Barnabas was selected by the apostles in Jerusalem to check it out. Guess who planted the church in Antioch? Men from Cyprus and Cyrene planted the church. Barnabas was a natural selection. He would have understood the perspectives and culture of the people who started the church. Barnabas' cross cultural sensitivity would have been learned when he lived in a bicultural setting in Cyprus. This cross cultural sensitivity would also have greatly enhanced the effectiveness of the early missionary journeys with Paul.

Thirdly, the generosity of Barnabas continued to be seen in the way that he taught the church in Antioch to respond to the need in Jerusalem. It is interesting to note that Paul watched Barnabas operate in the church in Antioch for a year and went with Barnabas to deliver the gift to the church in Jerusalem. Paul took on this value himself and encouraged all the churches that he started to be generous in their giving. He himself took up a collection for the church in Jerusalem many years later.

Can you see the sovereign hand of God shaping, planning, preparing Barnabas for his role?

What about you?

How can you learn to see the sovereign hand of God tracing through your own past? If you've come from a negative situation, it will be harder for you to see God's hand. Pray and ask God to lead you. It can be one of the most healing times that you can go through. There are a number of things that can help you begin to identify the things that God was doing in your upbringing to prepare you for your future role. I am going to mention just two of these.

Family Influence

Whether you perceive your family influence to be positive or negative, you can learn to see the hand of God. Begin by identifying how you were shaped by your families influence.

What kind of values did you learn?   How did you learn to perceive people and situations around you?   If you begin to think back on your family's influence, you will find that God used both positive and negative circumstances to shape your character and personality.

I remember talking with a girl who had grown up in a horrible family setting. Her parents were involved in satanic rituals and abused her in every conceivable way.   She had recently come to Christ and had listened to me share about learning to see God's sovereign hand in your past and celebrating the uniqueness that God had given to each person. After the session, she came up to me and was quite angry. She shared her background briefly and said that there was no way that God was sovereignly involved. I had to admit that I really couldn't disagree with her when I heard some of her stories. However, I shared two things with her. First, I told her that more time and more healing from God would give her a better chance to see her history from God's perspective. Secondly, I asked her how many people she had run across since the time that she had been saved that had encountered similar situations in their past.   She said that she ran across people like that all the time. I asked her how she felt inside when she heard their stories.   She said that it made her angry on the one hand and yet it made her hurt inside because she wanted to help them because she knew the kind of pain that they were going through. As she was talking, her anger subsided a little but not completely.   She began to see the light in some small way. I encouraged her to be patient and press deeply into the loving arms of her Savior. I encouraged her to pursue the love of God and its healing power with everything she had.   Finally, I encouraged her to share what she learned with others who struggled with similar experiences in their own past.

I don't know what has happened to the young woman since that day but I pray that she pressed deeply into God. As the love of God penetrates and heals the wounds within her, some of that anger will dissipate and I believe that she will begin to see that horrendous past in the light of His love.

Basic Skills

Another way to see the sovereign hand of God in your past is to look at the basic abilities or skills that you inherited genetically or learned because of your surroundings. Often, the basic skills which we learned while growing up are used later by God in powerful ways.

One of my favorite missionary stories is that of J.O. Fraser. As he was growing up, he found that he loved to climb mountains. He loved the physical challenge and the isolation. There was a sense of accomplishment that he relished. When God called him to go to China as a missionary, he gave J.O. Fraser a vision to reach the Lisu people. Guess where they lived...in the steep mountains in the south western region of China. If you read his biography, you will learn that J.O. Fraser climbed up and down those mountains in order to share the love of Christ with the remote tribes. He loved to climb mountains.

Pressing Ahead

I am so glad that God chose to use a person like the apostle Paul in such a mighty way. One of the things that I like best about Paul is that he was extremely genuine in his love for people. He was brutally honest about himself. He gave God all the glory while pursuing Him and His ministry with everything that he had.

Earlier in this chapter I made the comment that a person's negative past can be a debilitating barrier to being released into effective ministry. It is also true that a positive past can also be a debilitating barrier. Whereas a negative and hurtful past tends to hinder an emerging leader through self-doubt, condemnation, and guilt, a positive past can hinder an emerging leader through conceit, pride and self-exaltation. Both need to be avoided.

Paul demonstrated this in a wonderful way. On the one hand, he had a wonderful background. He had all the right credentials. He was born an Israelite and followed the law zealously as a trained Pharisee. No one could top his credentials. At the same time, he persecuted the church in his zealousness. He was aware that God had chosen him "the worst sinner" to be His apostle to the Gentiles. Paul demonstrated a certain attitude that it would be wise to follow as well. In Philippians 3:7 he says that "all the things that I might count as profit (his rich Jewish heritage) I now reckon as loss for Christ's sake." He goes on to say in verse 13 and 14, "The one thing I do, however, is to forget what is behind me and do my best to reach what is ahead. So I run straight toward the goal in order to win the prize, which is God's call through Christ Jesus to the life above."

Paul was fully aware of his past and how it impacted him. He was able to look back and see the sovereign hand of God. He did not ignore his past. Rather, on the basis of the past, he pressed ahead. He set his sights on running straight toward the goal that God had set before him.

How do you relate to your past? Does it hinder you in your relationship to God? How does your past influence the way you perceive yourself as a leader? I believe that we should follow the example of Paul. We should be able to look at our past and see the sovereign hand of God. This is especially true the older we get. We should celebrate what God has done and how He has used both the negative and positive influences and situations in our past. We need to recognize that God has been sovereignly involved in shaping us. Each one of us has a uniqueness before him. We need to discover that sense of uniqueness and celebrate what God has done in our past.

In the next few chapters, we are going to look specifically at how God shapes and influences us through changing our inner character. While we learn to celebrate our sense of uniqueness in personality, in experiences and in life history, we need to recognize that God is in the process of transforming us. In the early stages of ministry, God focuses on character formation.

Think back to the opening illustration. Can you understand why I have such confidence and enthusiasm concerning every emerging leader? I can't wait to discover how God wants to use each leader in unique ways to further the purposes of His Kingdom. It doesn't matter what kind of background you have come out of. God wants to use that background as a testimony to His faithfulness, His love, His mercy as He empowers you to influence others.

Evaluation and Application

1. When you think about your past, what kind of impressions do you have? Do you try to avoid thinking about it? Do you thank God for it?

2. When you think about the "sovereignty of God", is this a positive concept or a negative one? What does the "sovereignty of God" mean to you?

3. Who has been the person who has had the deepest ministry in your life? Was it a person who could identify with you and you felt that they understood you?

4. Thinking about your own background and beginnings, what important lessons have you learned that you could pass on to others?

4

Integrity:
The Foundation of Character

In the next two chapters, I (Paul) am going to write about character formation. During the first ten years of ministry, character formation is the primary focus of God as He develops His leaders. Our leadership development revolves around the issue of character development. We as emerging leaders need to respond to God's shaping hand and allow Him to transform our character. Effective ministry will flow out of a life that is firmly established in Godly character. If we do not embrace and learn these lessons of character, we will plateau in our growth. We will be frustrated in our efforts to develop as leaders. We will enter what I call a "crisis of intimacy". Let me describe a time in my own life in which I faced this kind of crisis.

A Crisis of Intimacy

The piece of paper before me listed the names of nine people. Beside each name was a description of my offense and the manner in which I was to contact them to admit my sin against them and ask for their forgiveness. Each time I looked at this paper I was filled with frustration, fear, and a sense of futility. How could I have allowed this to happen?

My early years as an adult had been filled with one "success" after another. After becoming a Christian in the early 1970's, I had been involved in happening churches and had been successful in ministry. I had attended seminary and graduate school and had achieved success as a professional. Everything I put my hand to seemed to prosper with hard work. There did not seem to be any task that I could not find a way to accomplish. By the time I was in my mid-thirties, I had accomplished my goals for education, employment and life-style.

But why was I so empty and bored? Why were the nagging difficulties that I had with my bosses in the past still bothering me? Why could I not find my niche in life and settle in for the long haul? Why was I always looking to the future and not able to enjoy the present? Why was I so restless?

All of these questions were merely symptoms and early warning signs of a shallow life, a life that did not have the internal resources necessary for faithfulness over the long haul. Unresolved issues from my past were beginning to pile up. The consequences of past choices were beginning to hinder my ability to cope with my life, my relationships, and my responsibilities.

Finally, I came to a place where I could no longer keep going in the direction that I had been going. Something major needed to take place. But what? When I compared myself with others, I looked pretty good. When I tried to analyze myself, I only got confused. I had learned how to rationalize and manipulate almost any situation and come out looking pretty good. But was looking good the real issue? I had grow suspicious of my motives, but how could I know for sure whether I was being selfish or just "acting in my own best interests"?

Through this process of evaluation, I discovered that my crisis was a crisis of relationship and integrity. I had based my life on the wrong things. Looking good had become more important than being the right kind of person. Covering up my "faults and mistakes" had become an obsession. I had not become a person of integrity.

During this time of personal turmoil and crisis, God began to take the initiative in giving me help and healing. He began to woe me (or more accurately He gave me the grace to recognize that He had been wooing me all along) and give me hope. I found myself asking, "is it possible after all I have done to turn my life around?" God's clear answer was "Yes! But it will be very costly. It will cost you everything that is not founded in relationship with me!"

And it did cost me. I sat and looked at the piece of paper in my hands. I responded to God in obedience and contacted the nine people listed and confessed my sin and asked for forgiveness. I was struck by how much my actions had hurt and damaged others and the reputation of Christ. Some of these people were still very angry with me and others were gracious and quickly extended forgiveness. Contacting these nine people was one of the hardest things that I have ever done in my life. But it set me on a course toward God that has turned my life around!

The Centrality Of Relationship

As I reflect on this crisis and God's solution to it, I am still overcome by the difficulty of it. However, I am overcome by the transformational power of the experience as well. I had discovered the reality that in order to live for Christ, you must die to yourself. This was not a new concept to me theologically. I had studied the concept in the Scriptures, listened to sermons about it, and read books on the subject. The problem was that I had never experienced it on an ongoing basis. This "crucified life" seemed too painful and felt out-of-control and risky for me.

My problem was that I had not abandoned control of my life to God on an ongoing basis, because I did not trust Him. Even though I had an orthodox theology, I did not have an orthodox lifestyle. The widening gap between what the Bible said and my life experience was beginning to tear me apart. Only a transforming relationship with God could bridge the widening gap. Vernon Grounds in his book *Radical Commitment* describes this transforming relationship in terms of the "Gethsemane mind-set". He writes that "it is the attitude of trustful self-surrender demonstrated by Jesus when He prayed, 'Not my will, Father, but your will be done.' It is the renunciation of our own very human feelings, desires, hopes, dreams, and ambitions in order that the purposes of God may be accomplished."[1]

At the center of Biblical Christianity is a trusting relationship with God. He can be trusted, even though His ways are not our ways (see Proverbs 3:5-8; Isaiah 55:8-13) He is good and the giver of good gifts (see Romans 8:28; James 1:17) The issue of trust is critical. Without it we will not be able to follow Him for very long because He asks us to walk by faith (in Him) not by sight (see 2 Corinthians 5:7; Hebrews 11).

How then is trust cultivated? Trust is cultivated by moving toward God, by spending time with Him, and by living according to His promises. As we get to know Him, we will trust Him more and as we trust Him more, we will get to know him more. This is risky business.

The first aspect of developing trust involves getting to know Him. As mentioned in chapter 2, the historical disciplines of the faith are avenues to building a trusting relationship with God. (see Figure 4-1: The Disciplines of the Faith) These inward, outward, and corporate disciplines allow us access to God and His loving grace.

Figure 4-1: Disciplines of the Faith

Inward	Outward	Corporate
Study	Simplicity	Confession
Meditation	Solitude	Guidance
Prayer	Submission	Worship
Fasting	Service	Celebration

Using these disciplines as avenues to building a trusting relationship with God can be tough at first. The proper exercise of the disciplines are contrary to our flesh. Intimacy with God exposes our true nature for what it is and most of us don't want to see ourselves in light of God's reality. Our flesh hates being exposed. Consequently, when you begin to approach God through the disciplines, you can expect that your flesh will want to rebel. Expect that your mind will be distracted or that circumstances will try to hinder or interfere with your scheduled time with God. In other words, expect resistance from within you as well as spiritual warfare against your efforts. This is all a regular part of building a trusting relationship with God. Expect it, press through it, and you will experience God in exciting and refreshing ways as the relationship deepens. Practicing the disciplines involves hard work which is why they are called "the disciplines".

Richard Foster, in his book *Celebration of Discipline* states that:

> "those who have heard the distant call [for intimacy with God] deep within and who desire to explore the world of the Spiritual Disciplines are immediately faced with two difficulties. The first is philosophic. The materialistic base of our age has become so pervasive that it has given people great doubts about their ability to reach beyond the physical world...the second difficulty is a practical one. We simply do not know how to go about exploring the inward life."[2]

I still remember my initial steps in developing a regular prayer life. I had been a "crisis oriented prayer warrior" for most of my Christian life and had never been able to cultivate a regular devotional prayer time. I felt that God had spoken to me that if I did not learn how to pray I would miss out on what He wanted to do in my generation. I did not want to miss out on what God was doing so I committed myself to developing a regular devotional prayer life.

Those first few days and weeks were so painful. I had no direction and I had set some unrealistic expectations. I was a miserable failure in my own eyes except that I did one thing right...I persevered. Those early attempts at prayer were very general and consisted primarily of a series of requests. After asking God to bless this thing or that event or to give me or them such and such, I would look at my watch and realize that only a few minutes had elapsed. I had committed myself to praying for 30 minutes. I didn't know what else to do during my prayer time.

Months later I looked back and discovered that I had made some progress. God had begun to meet me in the prayer times. He was beginning to teach me how to pray according to His will (see Luke 11:1-13). I had begun to experience something new during the prayer times. God was beginning to speak to me. I began to experience times of intimacy and gradually a whole new reality of the Christian life began to open up for me. Prayer time became a dialogue. Prayer time was a time of relationship building. It became rich and exciting. I looked forward to my time with God in a whole new way.

This process did not just happen. It involved a lot of hard work on my part. There are ups and downs in the process. There are still times when prayer seems dry. But the benefits of the hard work and a willingness to embrace prayer as a relationship building time has paid off. It is worth it!

We will not say much more about practicing spiritual disciplines in this book. There are a number of excellent books that are available on the subject. These books will assist you in developing a regular practice of the disciplines and will help you as you build your relationship with God. You will find a list of these books in Appendix 2.

The bottom line is that the cultivation of a devotional life is critical. Whatever strategy you develop will require time and effort on your part. There will be distractions and interruptions. Your flesh will rebel and the enemy will fight you. Expect all of this and persevere. Just do it. God loves you and is waiting.

The other aspect of developing trust is obedience. Trust will be reflected in our level of obedience. Peter is a wonderful example of this. One night he and the disciples were crossing the Sea of Galilee when they saw Jesus walking on the water (Matthew 14). At first they thought that Jesus was a ghost. Jesus spoke to them and Peter responded, "Lord, if it is you...tell me to come to you on the water." Jesus' response was "come". (verse 28-29) At this point, Peter had a decision to make. He could stay in the boat and make some excuse for not responding. He could swim out to where Jesus was or he could try to walk on the water. The parallel between Peter's options and our own options in situations that require faith and obedience are similar. Peter decided to try to walk! He knew that walking on the water was impossible. But he went for it. He got out of the boat and began to walk on the water. When he took his eyes off of Jesus and felt the wind and saw the waves around him, he began to sink. As he began to sink, he cried out, "Lord, save me." Jesus reached out his hand and caught him.

Even though Jesus rebuked Peter for his lack of faith (verse 31), Peter had learned a great lesson of faith. I can not but think that Jesus was also thinking, "Way to go Peter! You are going to make it. I am looking for someone who is willing to take risks to help me build my church." After all, we need to remember that Peter was the only one who got out of the boat. He was the only one who walked on the water. Even though the others must have learned from Peter's experiment, Peter experienced God's supernatural enabling to do the impossible!

This story is a very human example of how we cultivate a trusting relationship with God. We move toward Him in obedience, regardless of circumstances and consequences. As we experience His supernatural enabling and experience His hand reaching out to rescue us, we grow to trust Him more and more. Paul speaks of the "righteousness of God [being] revealed from faith to faith..." (Romans 1:17 KJV) As we exercise our faith in God we realize more fully that He is faithful!

The Importance of Integrity

In my crisis, I recognized that I was desiring a deeper intimacy with God. Relationship with God is the foundation of ministry. Integrity is the foundation of Godly character. I realized that my journey deeper into relationship with God was going to involve learning to walk in integrity. The list of names and the issue of confession and reconciliation represented a movement toward a life of integrity.

Integrity is a byproduct of a trusting relationship with God. As we learn to trust Him for the fundamentals of life, we can begin to trust Him for the radical surgery of the heart that leads to a life of integrity and Christlikeness.

Integrity involves "the quality or state of being complete or undivided" and involves a consistency between what we claim to believe and what we are and what we do.[3] Integrity is very similar to the New Testament concept of purity. Purity involves freedom from impure mixtures, being without blemish, or being spotless.[4] Basically, integrity means that "what you see is what you get." My life ought to be a pure expression of what I believe regardless of circumstances or consequences. Our lives are to be pure with no compromise!

In James 1:2-4 we are told that trials and difficulties provide a context for integrity to be developed. James says, "Consider it pure joy, my brothers, whenever you face trials of many kinds, because you know that the testing of your faith develops perseverance. Perseverance must finish its work so that you may be mature and complete, not lacking anything."

Notice a couple of things about trials in this passage. First, we are to consider them from a perspective of joy. J.P. Phillips, in his translation of this passage, says, "consider trials as friends". What? How is this possible? It is possible because trials provide a context for the testing of our faith. Trials can produce something good!

The second thing to notice about trials is that they provide an opportunity for growth. The testing of our faith is similar to the process of purifying precious metals. The raw ore is placed in a crucible and heated. As the raw ore melts a separation takes place and the impurities rise to the surface. These impurities are then drawn off which leaves the remaining ore more pure. This process is repeated until the ore is declared sterling or 100% pure. In the early days of metal working, ore was declared sterling when the craftsman could see his own reflection perfectly in the surface of the molten ore.

The imagery of this purification process gives us a vivid picture of the Christian life. It gives us a vivid picture of integrity. What you see is what you get! But what you see had to go through the process of purification. We too have to go through a process which allows us to learn to walk in integrity. God uses what we call integrity checks to teach us to walk in integrity.

Integrity Checks

An integrity check "refers to the special kind of process test which God uses to evaluate heart intent, consistency between inner convictions and outward actions, and which God uses as a foundation from which to expand the [Christian's] capacity to influence." [5]   From the moment that we commit our lives to Christ, we are in the process of being transformed. God through the power of the Holy Spirit, transforms and shapes our character to be like His. We are becoming Christlike. The character lessons related to integrity are the crucial lessons to learn. During the early stages of ministry, God takes each leader through a number of integrity checks to teach the leader to walk in integrity.

In Bobby Clinton's research, he has observed a number of different kinds of integrity checks. Along with identifying these different kinds of integrity checks, he has identified many ways that God uses them and the kind of benefit that leaders receive as they go through them. We are going to look at the different integrity issues individually.

Temptation

Temptation is the most common form of an integrity check. It is interesting to note that the same word in the New Testament for testing is also translated temptation in some passages. Dave Roper in his book on James entitled *The Law That Sets You Free!* explains the double use of testing/temptation this way, "a test is an experience which God brings into our life in order to build us. A temptation comes from Satan. It is designed to cause us to sin. But the amazing thing is that any experience can be either a test or a temptation, depending upon our response to it." [6]

The Bible gives us some further insight into the nature of temptations and how we can overcome them. First, temptation is common to all people and is resistible (see 1 Corinthians 10:13). Second, temptation is not from God (James 1:13). And third, Jesus has faced whatever temptation we might face without giving in to it. Consequently, he can help us as we face it. (see Hebrews 2:18; 4:15-16)

Temptation has a pattern that can be discerned and we can learn how to appropriate the power of the Holy Spirit to resist temptation and overcome it. James 1:14-15 describes the pattern of temptation in the following way,

"...but each one is tempted when by his own evil desire, he

is dragged away and enticed. Then, after desire has conceived, it gives birth to sin, and sin, when it is full-grown, gives birth to death."

Temptation in this passage involves an enticement of our own fleshly desires (stage 1). Sin occurs when these desires are conceived with our will (stage 2). And death, either spiritual, personal, or relational is the ultimate result of sin (stage 3). Understanding this pattern can help us learn how to resist temptation and not give in to sin.

Figure 4-3: The Pattern of Temptation/Sin

"Desire"	"Sin"	"Death"
—————————>	—————————>	—————————>
Stage 1	Stage 2	Stage 3
The Flesh	The Will	Spiritual, personal or relational

The time between Stage 1 and Stage 2 is the critical point for our understanding of how to resist temptation. The desire is not sin. Giving ourselves over to the desire is the sin. The desire comes from the flesh or the sinful nature. We have the Holy Spirit living within us who enables us to be righteous. The choice is ours! The choice may not be easy. We may have patterns of sin in our life that are deeply rooted (see 2 Corinthians 10:4-6). We may even enjoy sin. Whatever the circumstances, sin still involves us giving our will over to the fleshly desires and as Christians, we do not have to do this any more. We can choose to say no to temptation!

The battle of temptation is usually won or lost in the mind. We tend to rationalize and/or flirt with desire in our mind prior to giving in to temptation. This is why the Bible focuses so much on the need to be transformed by the renewal of our minds (see Romans 12:2). Other similar passages exhort us to bring "every thought captive to the obedience of Christ" (see 2 Corinthians 10:5 NASV). We are to put on the "helmet of salvation" (see Ephesians 6:17) and we are to have the same attitude (mind) as Christ (Philippians 2:5). Finally, we are to be renewed in the spirit of our minds (see Ephesians 4:23) and are exhorted to have the mind of Christ (see 1 Corinthians 2:16).

Neil Anderson, in his book, *The Bondage Breaker*, describes this battle for the mind when he states that,

> "just because you are now a Christian, don't think that Satan is no longer interested in manipulating you to his purposes through your mind. Satan's perpetual aim is to infiltrate your thoughts with his thought and to promote his lie in the face of God's truth. He knows that if he can control your thoughts, he can control your behavior."[7]

Temptation can be resisted. We can break sinful patterns. We must learn to resist temptation and overcome sin if we are to develop a mature and victorious Christian life. In integrity checks involving temptation, we need to learn to choose the Godly response in the situation.

Restitution

True confession and repentance may also involve restitution if we have stolen something. If we have damaged a relationship, we need to offer reconciliation. Restitution and reconciliation are often proofs of true confession and are an important part of "righting the wrong". As in my case, God tested the sincerity of my confession. I told God that I would do anything to draw closer to Him and He asked me to reconcile some past relationships. He confronted me with my sin towards others. I really struggled with this. Fortunately, God would not let me off the hook until I finally contacted everyone on the list. And thank God that I did. This act of confession on my part paved the way back to intimacy with God and a sense of integrity.

If you have ever been in the position of having to make restitution or seek reconciliation, you understand how difficult this can be. It will make a lasting impression on you. It will serve as a vivid reminder of the impact of sin and may act as a deterrent to further sinful behavior on your part.

Paul instructed Timothy that the "goal of our instruction is love from a pure heart and a good conscience and a sincere faith." (1 Timothy 1:5, NASV) Love is the goal and it comes from three qualities in the Christian: a pure heart, a good conscience and a sincere faith.

For our purposes here, let us look at the quality of a good conscience. A good conscience is critical for the welfare of the Christian. The alternative to a good conscience is a guilty conscience. Unresolved sin produces a guilty conscience. Unresolved sin also produces spiritual, personal, and relational death. We have difficulty approaching God because we are sinful. We have difficulty accepting ourselves and relating to others when we have a guilty conscience.

Jesus told his disciples that the prince of the world (Satan) had no hold on Him (John 14:30). Unresolved sin gives the enemy a hold in our life. Jesus was able to resist Satan's attempts to gain an advantage against Him because there was no sin. Jesus has made provision for us to live in the same reality. We need to learn to do whatever it takes to resist sin and resolve it quickly when we do fall. This will enable us to live with a good conscience.

How badly do we want to be right with God? Do we want to be right with Him badly enough to root out sin? Are we willing to make restitution and pursue reconciliation when our situation calls for it? God may ask this of us as a proof that we are willing to make things right. Gaining integrity and living in integrity may involve restitution and reconciliation.

Value Checks

A value check is a God initiated set of circumstances designed to test and clarify values for growth and the expansion of ministry. As we develop in ministry, we will operate from a set of values. Values define priorities and important beliefs. In this type of integrity check, God may place us in circumstances where we have to choose a course of action that demonstrates our values.

Maintaining integrity in relationship to our values is important. God will allow circumstances which check whether or not we are willing to back down or stand firm on our values.

We often do not really know what our values are until there is pressure on us in a certain situation. Our values will guide us in our behavior. For example, we may say that serving others is a value. God will put us in a situation where we get to serve with absolutely no recognition from others. How do we respond? Do we serve willingly and what is our attitude? Integrity in relationship to values means that our actions and attitudes are consistent with what we believe is important. It is important for us to discover our core values so that if they are not in line with the character of Christ, we can change them. It is much better for this process to take place early in life before we have major responsibilities and larger temptations.

Loyalty

There are many popular leadership teachings concerning authority and loyalty. In some circles, loyalty to one's leader is equated with loyalty to God. In other circles, loyalty to God and God alone is stressed to the detriment of God's leaders.

The Bible is clear that our ultimate loyalty must be to God (see Exodus 20:1-7 and Matthew 22:34-40). It is also clear that we are to submit to leaders that God has appointed over us. This submission includes governmental leaders (Romans 13:1), church leaders (1 Peter 5:5), in marriage relationships (Ephesians 5:22) and includes submitting to one another in the body of Christ (Ephesians 5:21). The Bible makes it clear that we are not to submit to leaders who are in violation of God's word (Acts 4:19-20). This issue of submission creates a certain tension for each one of us. We need to press into God and search His word and ask the Holy Spirit to guide us in each situation.

An integrity check involving the issue of loyalty whether it is to God or others is difficult. Loyalty is based on trust. Trust is the key issue. The development of loyalty to God and God's leaders in spite of their imperfections is critical for character development. Integrity in this situation is maintaining a loyalty to God and His chosen leaders.

Guidance

Guidance from God is critical for a Christian. Without guidance, we do not know what to do or where to go. In Proverbs 29:18 we learn that "where there is no revelation, the people cast off restraint." The reverse could be stated as well, "where there is revelation, there is direction!"

Integrity and guidance are closely related, because guidance involves not only hearing God but obeying God. It is not enough to hear God. We must also obey Him. (see Matthew 7:24-27) If we do not obey God once we have heard Him, we are in sin and this will result in difficulty in hearing from God. When we confess our disobedience, we will be able to hear from God again.

Here is one way that I have seen God check a person's integrity in a guidance situation. The person feels that they have gotten a sense of direction or guidance from God on some issue. Before he/she can act on that guidance, another "more attractive" offer comes up. Will we maintain our integrity and follow through on what we believed God had shown us at first or will we go with the more attractive alternative? Integrity means following through on what we believe God has revealed to us in the guidance situation.

Conflict Against Ministry Vision

When God gives a person direction regarding ministry, we call this ministry vision. One of the ways that God tests a person's integrity is by giving a person some direction for ministry and then bringing conflict against that vision. The conflict can come through circumstances or people. God is looking to see how the person will respond to the conflict. A person of integrity will persevere and push through the conflict until God meets him/her. A person lacking integrity will quit or give up. The real issue involved in these types of integrity checks is faith. Will the person believe what God has shown him/her no matter what?

If we will be faithful, conflicts involving ministry vision can lead to a refining of vision, character development, and new opportunities for ministry. If not, these conflicts can lead to hurt, confusion, and bitterness that can have a negative impact on yourself and others. God is looking for people of integrity who will follow through on a commitment.

Leadership Backlash

Leadership backlash is a special kind of conflict in ministry. It happens when a leader is attempting to implement a new direction in the ministry. Initially the people who are involved respond enthusiastically and with support. Over time, a few problems begin to emerge as the changes are implemented. At this time, people reverse their support and often fight against the new direction. The leader who is attempting to implement the change is caught in the backlash.

This type of scenario will certainly test the integrity of the leader in many ways. Will he/she stay focused on what God started or will he/she back down or give up? Moses faced a tremendous leadership backlash in the desert with the people of Israel. Moses was highly supported and looked up to when he led the people out of Egypt. However, at the first sign of trouble or adversity, the leaders and the people of Israel wanted to abandon Moses' leadership and go back to Egypt. He stayed focused on God's agenda and continued to lead them toward the promised land. Even though he must have been personally hurt by their rejection, he stayed loyal to them. He maintained his integrity!

As a leader or follower, we may experience the pressures and stresses that come during the implementation of a vision or new program in ministry. Few plans are ever implemented without some difficulty. When unforeseen difficulties arise people may become unhappy, confrontational, divisive, and/or quit. In cases such as these, our response is critical. Patience, forgiveness, re-evaluation, and/or change in certain aspects of implementation may be necessary. How will you respond?

Persecution

Persecution is not a very popular concept in our contemporary Christian subculture. We believe that material and situational blessing is the lot of the obedient Christian. But this is only part of the Biblical understanding of obedience. Hard as it may seem for many of us to believe, persecution is also the lot of the obedient Christian.

Jesus is the paramount example of this. He lived in total obedience (Hebrews 4:15-16). He experienced both the blessing of God and persecution. In fact, He taught his disciples, "blessed are those who are persecuted because of righteousness..." (Matthew 4:10). In other passages, He shared that persecution is inevitable for the obedient Christian (see Mark 10:30 and John 15:20).

Persecution comes in many ways. It can be overt, such as political and/or legal opposition. It can be subtle, such as social pressure to conform to non-Biblical standards. Whatever the form, persecution will probably come and the Christian must not be surprised or offended by it. Persecution can serve as an opportunity for growth and effective testimony.

Shadrach, Meshach and Abednego were persecuted for their obedience when they did not bow down to the golden image that Nebuchadnezzar had created (see Daniel 3). They were arrested and sentenced to be burned to death in a furnace. But when Shadrach, Meshach, and Abednego were thrown into the furnace, they were suddenly accompanied by a fourth person who "looks like a son of the gods". (verse 25). They were not consumed by the fire and upon their release from the furnace were promoted. The God of Israel received great honor. What a picture of the benefits of faithfulness in times of persecution!

Persecution can also be used by God to expose the nature of our commitment to Him. In the parable of the sower, Jesus said that one of the groups received the word with joy (the rocky soil). However, when persecution came because of the word, they quickly fell away.

By contrast, James encouraged believers who were suffering under persecution to take it as blessing. He writes, "blessed is the man who perseveres under trial; because when he has stood the test, he will receive the crown of life that God has promised to those who love Him." (James 1:12)

Persecution can reveal the level of commitment that we have to God. Are we willing to pay the price to follow Christ? No one likes persecution, but it can be the "fire" that purifies and serves as a witness to a world looking for someone who will stand up for what they believe even if it costs them (see 1 Peter 2:12). Persecution provides a tremendous opportunity to maintain and grow in our integrity.

Uses and Benefits of Integrity Checks

Bobby Clinton has identified seven primary uses and benefits to going through integrity checks. He lists them as follows:
1. to see whether or not we will follow through on promise or a vow that we made to God.
2. to create or insure a sense of burden for a ministry vision or the ministry itself.
3. to promote inner character growth and strength of character.
4. to build our faith in God.
5. to help establish inner values and convictions that will be important to our future leadership.
6. to teach us submission.
7. to warn others of the seriousness of following God.[8]

We will all go through integrity checks. Integrity is an essential quality for every Christian leader who wants to have Godly character. God will initiate many different scenarios in which our integrity will be tested. Our response is crucial. We can learn to walk in integrity. Walking in integrity will keep us close to God. For me, the journey deeper into God began with the issue of integrity in past relationships. As difficult as that experience was, I thank God that He is faithful to me as I endeavor to walk in integrity.

Evaluation and Application

1. Prayerfully ask God to lead you to the relational aspect or integrity check that He would like you to focus on.

2. Reread that section or sections and look up all of the supporting passages while asking God to reveal Himself and his purposes to you.

3. Write down your insights and ask God how he wants you to apply these insights.

4. Write down a strategy for applying these insights, act on them, and evaluate.

5. If you discover that you need to make restitution or seek reconciliation, ask God for a specific approach and prayerfully follow through.

[1] Vernon Grounds, Radical commitment, Portland, OR: MUltonomah Press, 1984, p.42

[2] Richard Foster, Celebration of Discipline, San Francisco: Harper and Row Publishers, 1978, 1988 p.2-3.

[3] Web ster's Seventh New Collegiate Dictionary G & G Merriam Company, 1967, p.439.

[4] W.E. Vine, Expository Dictionary of New Testament Words, Old Tappan, NJ: Fleming H. Revell, 1966, p. 194, 231-232.

[5] J. Robert Clinton, Leadership Emergance Theory, Altadena, CA: Baranbas Publishers, 1989, p. 125.

[6] David H. Roper, The Law That Sets You Free!. Waco, TX: Word, 1977, p. 53.

[7] Neil Anderson, The Bondage Breaker, Eugene, OR: HArvest House, 1990, p.53.

[8] Clinton, The Making of a Leader, p. 127-140

5

Hearing and Obeying the Voice of God

We (Paul and his family) had just returned to the United States after spending the summer in Mexico helping coordinate short-term outreaches for North American young people. The summer had been challenging and rewarding as we saw God work in the lives of the Mexican people and the young people on outreach.

We had seen God work through cultural barriers, diversity of church denominations, and differences in personalities. People got saved, some got healed, construction projects were completed, and young people were challenged with the realities of world missions. It had been a dynamic summer.

But all this had come at a cost. We had lived in a one-bedroom apartment, struggled with sickness, experienced cultural shock, wrestled with spiritual warfare, and faced our own human limitations. Now we had returned to our base in the United States to find out that our financial support during the summer had fallen off to almost nothing.

We were members of a "faith mission". We had felt that we had been given "clear" direction from God that while we were with this mission organization, we were not to raise support but to make our needs known only to God in prayer. This had worked well for the first year but now we were faced with limited finances and growing financial needs.

During the summer we discovered that my wife Leslie was pregnant with our third child. We were excited about this but our catastrophic health insurance plan did not cover pregnancies. What were we going to do?

On top of this, we sensed that God was "asking" us to give from our limited savings to a needy co-worker and some other mission enterprises. *Was this really God?* Were we hearing from Him or were we experiencing the side effects of a bad burrito from our recent mission's experience? How were we to know for sure? The pressures were great and we were afraid. We had never been this far out on the limb (or on the water) of faith before.

After discussing our options we decided that we needed clarity from God that usually only comes through waiting prayer. So we waited upon God in prayer individually for a couple of days. Through this process we experienced a growing sense that God had us right were He wanted us and that we were to give and trust Him.

I can still remember gathering the family together for an emergency prayer meeting the evening after writing and sending the checks off. I said, "Well folks, it's time for us to pray and for God to provide!" And we prayed and went to bed.

The next day I had an appointment to meet with several youth pastors in the community where we were based. After the meeting one of the pastors asked if he could talk with me. As we talked he gave me an envelope and said, "My mother prays for you and yesterday she had a real burden for you. She asked me to give you this as soon as possible."

When I opened the envelope there was a note of encouragement and a check for $500. God had already begun to provide as we had been struggling with obeying His word of faith. God's provision did not stop with this envelope. Within a month over $8000 came in without anybody knowing our situation. Again and again, we received letters of encouragement from people who were praying for us. Many of these letters also contained checks. *God was proving Himself faithful to His word.*

This story, as dramatic as it was, is an example of Biblical Christianity. Out of relationship with God and a life of integrity, we hear God's voice and as we obey we will see His provision! This kind of "faith" walk ought to be part of every Christian's experience. If you are an emerging leader, I can guarantee that God will lead you through numerous situations which He will use to check your development in the areas of hearing His voice, obeying His voice and operating in faith.

God initiates this type of shaping activity early in a believer's life. From the very first moments in our relationship with God, we begin to learn to communicate with Him. We begin to develop a sensitivity to His voice. The practicing of spiritual disciplines can help in this process. God will lead us through numerous situations during which we can learn to discern His voice. We call these incidents *word checks*.

In the last chapter, we looked at the importance of integrity. In this chapter, we will be looking at the relationship between learning to hear God's voice and the characteristic of obedience. Both of these are directly related to the development of faith. Faith checks involve our acting on the basis of something we believe God has told us. God uses word checks, obedience checks and faith checks to develop the foundational character that He can use in the future.

During the first ten years of ministry, this focus on learning to hear, learning to obey and learning to operate in faith is extremely important. Obedience along with integrity are critical elements of Godly character. Jesus modeled the relationship between hearing and obeying to perfection. Intimacy with His Father enabled Jesus to say that He only did the things that He saw the Father doing. He only spoke the words that His Father gave Him to say. (see John 5:19-20 & John 8::28) We can learn to operate in the same way that Jesus did. Jesus prays in John 17 that we might be one with Him in the same way that He and the Father are one. The Holy Spirit lives within us and enables us to operate in this union life with God.

The real problem for many of us is that we have not cultivated what Larry Lea has called the "hearing ear." We are not able to consistently distinguish God's voice from all the other voices and noises that we hear in our daily lives. And when we do hear God's voice, we are often afraid to obey because we lack trust in

God's ability to come through. In order for us to consistently go on with God, we need to learn how to hear and obey his voice.

The Voice of God - Revelation

Revelation refers to "God's self-disclosure to men and women. It is translated from a Greek word that means the drawing back of a veil to reveal hidden things."[1] Revelation involves God's initiative in revealing truth to man that he could not otherwise know. According to Christian theology, revelation involves two types of initiatives by God. The first is called general revelation and the second type is called special revelation.

General Revelation

General revelation includes God revealing Himself through nature (Psalms 19:1-4) and an internal revelation in each individual(Romans 1:19). In both of these realms, there is the witness of God and His power.

Natural revelation involves a general witness of the creative capacity of God in nature. James Montgomery Boice in this book *Foundations of the Christian Faith* states that "the revelation of God in nature is sufficient to convince anyone of God's existence and power, if the individual will have it."[2]

Internal revelation involves an inner witness and capacity to know God. Men and women are internally governed by a sense of right and wrong (even though they may not live consistently with these values). This sense of right and wrong ("conscience") points to a moral source (God) greater than man.

Although general revelation is not enough to provide the specific information about God that is necessary for relationship with Him, it does point the way for any who seek Him. An article on "revelation" in Baker's Encyclopedia of the Bible (Elwell, editor) states that:

"Natural knowledge of God, however, has its limitations, and its inadequacies. Because it confronts the individual with the fact of God's existence, the individual consequently engages in religious practice and asks some of the ultimate questions concerning the source, reason, and end of his or her own existence. But the tragic thing is, as Paul writes (Romans 1:18, 2:16), that since the fall people turn knowledge of God into perverse practices, worshipping not him, but images, creatures, or created things. Thus sinners drift further from God and satisfy themselves with foolish answers for the ultimate questions of existence."[3]

There is a need for more specific revelation if man is to find God and develop relationship with Him. Thus God has provided another type of revelation called special revelation. Without special revelation mankind would be caught in the dilemma of general knowledge of God without having specific knowledge necessary to find him.

Special Revelation

Special revelation includes the Bible (II Timothy 3:16), the person of Christ (Colossians 2:8-15), and the Holy Spirit (John 16:13). It is through the Bible, the person of Christ, and the Holy Spirit that humanity can know the specific way (see John 14:6) to build relationship with God.

The Bible is the history of God's plan of redemption and the standard of truth and faith. II Timothy 3:16-17 says that "all scripture is God-breathed ["inspired" in the KJV] and is useful for teaching, rebuking, correction, and training in righteousness, so that the man of God may be thoroughly equipped for every good work."

The Bible is "God-breathed" or "inspired." It is not mankinds words about God but God's word to mankind (see II Peter 1:20-21). Consequently, the Bible is authoritative. It is the truth and it is profitable! If we live by its standards we will realize its promise of righteousness ["right relationship"] and be equipped for every good work.

The Bible reveals the truth about God in several ways. First, the Bible teaches us about God. Teaching involves a basic explanation of the meaning of God's revealed truth in the Bible. Teaching also involves information about how to apply this truth in our daily lives. The teaching function of the Bible is designed to inform and transform. God desires that we know about Him and that we also know Him. This truth needs to be understood and applied.

Second, the Bible can rebuke us when we are in error personally or relationally. Rebuking involves conviction of error in either attitude or life-style. The Bible provides a standard for attitude (see Matthew 5-7) and behavior (see Exodus 20). When our attitudes and/or behaviors are contrary to Biblical standards then we need to change. The purpose of a rebuke is to turn one back to compliance with truth.

Third, the Bible can correct us when we are in error doctrinally. Correction involves the authoritative nature of the Bible as the final standard of doctrine and faith. The Bible is to be our authoritative source for truth, not our experience or our opinions. The Bible then is the standard by which we judge our experience and our opinions. If our experience and/or opinions differ from the clear teaching of the Bible, then we need to "correct" them.

Last, the Bible can train us in righteousness. Training involves the training of a child, including instruction and discipline. This type of training is relationally based (not program based). It involves learning within the context of submission to an authority. The Bible is a relational truth that trains us in relationship, character, and conduct.

The person of Christ is another source of special revelation. He is the "fullness of the Deity... in bodily form": (Colossians 2:9). He "being in very nature God..." became a man (Philippians 2:6-7). Christ is "the radiance of God's glory, and the exact representation of His being, sustaining all things by His powerful word" (Hebrews 1:3). Through His sinless life, death, and resurrection He has revealed the love of God for fallen man (see John 3:16) and the way of reconciliation (see Romans 5:10-11). The life of Christ reveals for us the love of God, the way of salvation, and the pattern for relationship.

The Holy Spirit is another source of special revelation. According to a section on "the Holy Spirit" in the *Topical Analysis of the Bible* (Elwell, editor) there are twenty-five distinct ministries of the Holy Spirit in the life of the believer mentioned in the Bible. These include,

1. Assistance in worship - Philippians 3:3
2. Assurance of salvation - Romans 8:16
3. Baptism into the body of Christ - I Corinthians 12:13
4. Blessing for believers - Galatians 6:8
5. Compels us towards God's will - Acts 20:22
6. Controls mind - Romans 8:5
7. Dwells in the believer - I Corinthians 3:16
8. Empowers - Acts 1:8
9. Equips for service - I Corinthians 12:7
10. Fellowship with believers - Philippians 2:1
11. Fights against the sinful nature - Galatians 5:17
12. Fills believers - Ephesians 5:18
13. Frees believers - Romans 8:2
14. A gift to believers - I John 4:13
15. Gives access to the Father - Ephesians 2:18
16. Glorifies Christ in the believer - John 16:13-14
17. Guarantees future blessing for believers - II Corinthians 5:5
18. Guides believers - Galatians 5:18, 25
19. Helps believers - Philippians 1:19
20. Prays for and with believers - Romans 8:26-27
21. Regenerates believers - Titus 3:5
22. Seals believers - Ephesians 1:13
23. Speaks through believers - Mark 13:11
24. Teaches believers - John 14:26
25. Transforms believers - II Corinthians 3:18 [4]

The role of the Holy Spirit in the life of the believer is vital. Learning to discern the Spirit (see I John 4:1-3) and appropriate all the resources that the Spirit represents is critical for our development as leaders.

The Holy Spirit, along with the Bible and the witness of Christ, form the foundation upon which we can learn to hear the voice of God for the daily decisions that we have to make as Christians. The Holy Spirit leads the believer to Christ and the truth of the

Bible. All three forms of special revelation compliment one another.

We Can Hear the Voice of God

Now that we have a basic idea of what the voice of God is, we can turn our attention to the specific task of learning to hear His voice. God has given us the Bible, Christ, and the Holy Spirit as sources of special revelation, but how do we know for sure that what we are reading, hearing, perceiving, and/or understanding is really God's voice? There are many different interpretations of Biblical passages. Some people speak of personal prophetic words, while still others challenge the authority of the Bible for personal morality. Is there a way to be sure about whether or not we are hearing God's voice?

Yes, there is! First of all, we need to remember that the Bible claims to be "inspired" (II Timothy 3:16) by a God of truth (Psalms 31:5). If it is, then it can be trusted (even if we have difficulty understanding some of it at times). Second, we need to remember that Jesus claimed to be the fulfillment of the Messianic prophecies of the Old Testament (Luke 4:21) and that He is the way, the truth, and the life (John 14:6). If He is, then He can be trusted. As we deepen our relationship with Him, we will know Him better and better. And third, we need to remember that the Bible and Jesus claimed that the Holy Spirit is the "Spirit of truth" (John 16:13). If this is true, then we can learn to trust the Holy Spirit to bring us to the truth of Christ and the Bible (see I John 4:1-3).

The primary issue involved in learning to hear and discern God's voice is trust. Are we going to lean on our own understanding (see Proverbs 3:5-6) or are we going to trust that God has provided us with the necessary resources to know Him? *Learning to hear God's voice must begin with a basic belief that God is trustworthy and that He has provided us with the means necessary to have a relationship with Him.* From this basis we can begin to relate to Him in ways that will lead to growth in character and effectiveness in ministry.

The Bible says that his sheep (believers) hear His voice (see John 10:4) and know Him (see John 10:14). As believers we can begin the process of learning to hear and discern God's voice with this confidence. His sheep hear His voice! They know Him! The Shepherd speaks to His sheep, leads them to food, water, and safety (see Psalms 23). The Shepherd even lays down His life for His sheep (see John 10:15). There is a relationship between these sheep and their Shepherd that involves communication.

Communication involves the accurate sending and receiving of information between people. Most of us have little difficulty with the sending part of communication. It is easy for us to make our needs know to others and/or to God. Where most of us have difficulty is in the receiving part of communication. We have a hard time listening to others and/or God. God has given us His Word, His Son, and His Spirit as resources and sources to know Him and know His will. But most of us have a difficult time knowing how to use these resources and sources in our daily lives.

Dick Eastman, in his "Challenge the World" School of Prayer seminars, gives fourteen principles of divine guidance that may be helpful in clarifying some of the confusion surrounding hearing the voice of God. These include,

1. It is possible to hear God's voice - Colossians 1:9
2. The purpose of all guidance is to know the Lord Jesus intimately - Philippians 3:20
3. God speaks from where He dwells - Luke 17:21
4. The Holy Spirit is heaven's representative in all true guidance - John 16:13
5. God's word is the final judge in all guidance - II Peter 1:19-20
6. Guidance from God is always accompanied by the peace of God - Philippians 4:6-7
7. God speaks through various means [Biblical examples in clude prayer, visitations, voices, visions, dreams, prophecy, circumstances, etc.]
8. Most guidance from God comes unawares - Psalms 25:9
9. There are several sources of guidance [see #7 above]
10. Hearing God speak must prompt us to action - James 2:17

11. Divine guidance comes from meeting God's demands - Isaiah 58:10-11
12. Divine guidance does not mean that we will know the future James 5:7-8
13. Guidance is not always pleasant - James 1:2-4
14. Guidance is a skill to be learned - Luke 11:1[5]

We see many of these principles illustrated in God's guidance of Paul during the initial stages of his "second" missionary journey (Acts 16). Paul and his companions traveled through Asia Minor delivering the decision reached by the Jerusalem council concerning the relationship of Gentile believers to the law and encouraging the churches (verses 1-5). Evidently Paul had the desire to take the gospel into Asia but the Holy Spirit would not allow them access (verses 6-7). Finally, while in Troas, Paul received a vision of a man of Macedonia standing and begging him to "come over to Macedonia and help us" (verses 8-9). After receiving this vision, Paul and his companions "got ready at once to leave for Macedonia, concluding that God had called [them] to preach the gospel to them" (verse 10).

In this passage we see that Paul and his companions were obeying the general call to "visit the brothers in all the towns where we [Paul and Barnabas on the "first" missionary journey] preached the word of the Lord and see how they are doing" (Acts 15:36). Once this was accomplished, Paul evidently decided to try to evangelize in the province of Asia (Acts 16:6) but was hindered by the Holy Spirit (Acts 16:6-7). This hindrance might have been circumstantial or spiritual, we do not know. But somehow the Spirit hindered Paul and used this hindrance to get him to Troas where he received a "vision" which lead him and his companions to Macedonia and later Greece (see Acts 16-18).

Notice the sovereign aspects of God's guidance even though Paul and his companions were not exactly sure where God was taking them. Also, notice that once they did know the specific will of God they responded immediately. Hearing the voice of God is a process based in relationship with a sovereign God who will reveal his purposes for us to obey.

Learning How to Hear the Voice of God

My wife Leslie and I (Paul) were at a crossroads in our life. I had left a very comfortable profession and life-style to "follow God wholeheartedly" but everything was turning out wrong. We were pretty sure that we had heard God about this decision, but why were not things working out?

During this time of frustration and doubt, God brought a man into our life for only a few minutes who would open up our eyes to the reality of living by faith and not by sight. He told my wife, "You are afraid of what might happen if you miss it [God's will]. What you should really be asking is "what might happen if I hit it!" There is a risk involved in learning how to hear the voice of God. But there is an incredible potential for the advance of the kingdom if we will face the risk and start asking, "what might happen if I hit it!"

Jesus said that "the kingdom of heaven has been forcefully advancing, and forceful men lay hold of it" (Matthew 11:12). The concept of force here could be translated "violence" and this verse could read "the kingdom of God has been violently advancing, and violent men lay hold of it." This kind of forcefulness or violence comes from a realization that there is a war going on and that only through risking one's life can the enemy be defeated. Following Jesus is a risky business, but at the same time, "what might happen if I hit it!"

Biblical faith (see II Corinthians 5:7) involves "being sure of what we hope for and certain of what we do not see" (Hebrews 11:1). What we hope for is God's will (see Psalms 37:4) and what we do not see is the future faithfulness of God. But it all involves taking a chance on God.

Learning how to hear the voice of God involves several basic steps. *First of all, we need to want to hear the voice of God.* The motivation of our heart is critical. If we are not open to the "control" of the Spirit (see Ephesians 5:18), we will "grieve" the Spirit (see Ephesians 4:30) and possibly even "quench" the spirit (see I Thessalonians 5:19 KJV). Without the desire to hear the voice of God, we will have difficulty hearing His voice on a regular basis and eventually we will find ourselves confused by the competing voices of the flesh, the world, and the enemy.

Second, we need to get to know Christ through the reading and studying of the word of God. Psalms 119 reveals for us the benefits of building our lives on the truth of the "law" of God. Jesus tells us that the "truth" will set us free (see John 8:32). Paul exhorted the younger Timothy to study the Word (II Timothy 2:15). Getting to know Christ through the Bible is the foundation on which we can discern whether what we are hearing is really from God or not.

There are many good books and resources on how to read and study the Bible. A good Bible with study helps might be a good place to start. Once you have an overview of the Bible you may begin to cultivate an interest in a specific book or topic. At this point you might want to seek the counsel of your pastor or an older Christian who might be able to point you toward some helpful books or resources. Good Bible teaching from your local church pastor and a small fellowship group might also be good resources as you get to know Christ better through your reading and study of the Bible.

Third, consistently obey the clear teaching of the Bible. The Bible says that, "this is love for God: to obey his commands. And his commands are not burdensome, for everyone born of God overcomes the world. This is the victory that has overcome the world, even our faith" (I John 5:3-4).

Obedience to the clear teaching of the Bible is critical for growth in relationship with God. We can know about Him through the teaching of the Bible, but we really get to know Him by obeying his commandments. Not only do we grow in our relationship with God through obedience, but we also remain open to His revelation. Without obedience, we become desensitized to His voice. Obedience to God's commands as revealed in His Scriptures will lead to intimacy with Him. Intimacy makes communication easier. Disobedience will lead to a distanced relationship and communication is more difficult.

David is an example of this. When he committed adultery with Bathsheba (II Samuel 11) and she became pregnant, he tried to cover up his sin by having Uriah called home from the front (verses 6-13) to sleep with his wife. When Uriah refused to sleep with his wife, David gave orders to have him murdered in battle (verses 14-17).

David's sin and his failure to confess it lead him to try to cover it up which in turn resulted in murder. He knew the law. He knew that adultery and murder were wrong, but sin lead to a desensitization towards God's word. It was not until the prophet Nathan confronted him with his sin (II Samuel 12) that he was able to finally confess it (see Psalms 51). Through confession, David was forgiven but there were severe consequences for him, his family, and the people he was supposed to lead in righteousness (see I Samuel 12:9-14).

Lack of obedience is disobedience and disobedience kills. If we want to have a vital relationship with God and hear his voice we must cultivate regular obedience to the clear teaching of the Bible. Obedience in these areas (the areas the Bible speaks about) prepares us for hearing and obeying God's voice in areas of specific guidance and application that are not clearly described in the Bible. It is important to see this connection. It is all about relationship with God and drawing closer to Him.

Fourth, learn to meditate on the word of God. Ask the Holy Spirit to reveal to you the meaning of specific Bible passages for your life (see John 16:12-15). Mark Virkler, in this book <u>Dialogue With God</u>, describes four keys to meditation based on the Habakkuk 2:1-3 passage.[6] The first key is the spoken word. Virkler describes this as learning what His voice spoken within sounds like. This inner voice will never contradict the teaching of the Bible. In actuality it is the Holy Spirit revealing specific application of truth to us consistent with the Bible and the person of Christ.

The second key is becoming still. Virkler describes this as going to a quiet place and quieting our emotions and thoughts so that we can hear God through His Spirit. This quieting does not mean that we abandon or deny our cognition and/or emotions, but that we intentionally submit them to God in such a way that they do not interfere with our communication with God.

The third key is seeing in the Spirit. Virkler describes this as focusing our heart (mind, emotions, will) upon Jesus with the intention of seeing as Jesus sees. During this process ideas, visions, and dreams may occur. These ideas, visions, and dreams are not necessarily the voice of God and they must be submitted to the standards of the Bible.

The fourth key is writing out dialogue with God. Virkler encourages journalling of the ideas, visions, and dreams that you believe come from seeing in the Spirit. Writing these things down can be a helpful way to remember and evaluate what we think we have heard from God and can be useful in helping us to grow in our ability to hear God's voice.

This is not the only format for meditation, but it is a helpful one. God will lead you in your process of meditation. Remember that all "personal" revelation must be submitted to the standard of the Bible. Wise counsel from other mature Christians can also be helpful in discerning whether or not what you heard is form God or not (see Proverbs 15:22).

Fifth, learn to discern the Spirit. The Holy Spirit lives in the believer (I Corinthians 3:16) and teaches us all truth and reminds us of the life and words of Christ (John 14:26). The Bible encourages us to test the spirits to see if they are from God (I John 4:1-3).

The Holy Spirit can and does reveal specific truth to us. He reminds us of a specific scripture. He reminds us of an incident in the life of Jesus. He gives us insight into the application of Scripture for specific areas of our life. He gives us insight into the needs of others for ministry purposes. All of these applications and many more are available to the believer as we learn to discern the Spirit.

The prayer teaching of Dick Eastman is again helpful at this point. He describes six dangers or errors in learning how to hear the voice of God or discern the Spirit. These include,

1. Assuming all guidance comes from God.
2. Thinking that God always uses spectacular means in guidance.
3. Basing all guidance on fleeces.
4. Valuing impressions, visions, and dreams above the Word.
5. Misunderstanding circumstances in relationship to guidance.
6. Ruling out the need for divine guidance.[7]

God may use some of these means to communicate to us but the danger comes when we presume that He will always communicate in a certain way. In the Bible we see that God has used diverse means to communicate with his people. We need to remain humble and open to God and allow him to communicate in whatever means God thinks best.

Remember that God's voice will never violate God's word. He will never ask us to sin in order to accomplish His righteous purposes! The voice of God through the Holy Spirit will always compliment the teaching of the Bible and the person of Christ. If we are hearing something that is in conflict with the Bible and/or the person of Christ, it is not from God!

Sixth, we need to step out in faith when we are reasonably sure that we have heard from God. There will be times in our Christian life when we might not be absolutely sure that what we are "hearing" is really from God. In cases like these we need to seek God for confirmation. Again, the Bible is the standard for initial judgment in these cases. If the message does not contradict the clear teaching of the Bible, it may be from God but often we may still need confirmation.

Gideon is probably one of the best known examples of this in the Bible (see Judges 6-8). Gideon was given the charge (by angelic visitation) of leading Israel against the Midianites (Judges 6:12-14). But Gideon was unsure about this "guidance" so he asked God for a "fleece" as confirmation (Judges 6:36-40). God confirmed His word through the fleece and Gideon obeyed God and defeated Midian (Judges 7).

In times of confusion and uncertainty, God will often times provide needed confirmation. He does not provide confirmation in every situation. There are times when He wants us to respond in faith. However, I have found that in big decisions or at important moments dealing with sensitive issues, it is wise to ask God for confirmation. Remember, asking God to confirm some decision or direction assumes that you have already be seeking God and have gotten an answer of some kind. In these situations, God will sometimes use people to bring confirmation. God brings mentors alongside us in critical moments. These types of mentors are called divine contacts. God uses them to confirm what He is doing or what He is saying. Ananias was a divine contact for Saul/Paul. Saul was sitting in Damascus after his dramatic encounter with Jesus on the road. He believed that he was receiving direction and guidance from God. But it was in diametrical opposition to the way that he was living his life. How could he be sure that it was really God? God spoke to Ananias and told him where to find Saul and to give a message. Ananias' words confirmed what Saul had been hearing himself. A little later, God brought Barnabas alongside Paul in order to give Paul credibility and acceptance into the mainstream of the young emerging church.

God also uses circumstances to provide confirmation of His direction and leading. On the missionary journeys, Paul, Barnabas and the other team members had their agendas set by the response of the people. Often times persecution would lead them to move on to the next city. Other times, their message was embraced and they stayed longer. God literally opened and closed doors for them.

One of the main things to remember is that God promises to provide wisdom for those who ask him for it (James 1:5). If we need wisdom, we need to ask believing that He will provide. If we need confirmation, God will provide it. We need to be aware of the many different ways that God brought confirmation to His leading in the Biblical accounts. This would make a great personal Bible study.

Once we are reasonably sure that we have heard from God we need to step out in faith. Stepping out in faith is what obedience is all about.

Obedience

We have already commented on the importance of obedience in relationship to hearing the voice of God. We must be willing to obey in order to hear and we must hear in order to know how to obey. Hearing and obeying are two sides of the same coin. They are connected.

James warned that faith without works is dead (James 2:17). He said,

> "What good is it, my brothers, if a man claims to have faith but has no deeds? Can such faith save him? Suppose a brother or sister is without clothes or daily food. If one

of you says to him, "Go, I wish you well; keep warm and well fed, " but does nothing about his physical needs, what good is it? In the same way, faith by itself, if not accompanied by action is dead. But someone will say, "You have faith, I have deeds." Show me your faith without deeds, and I will show you my faith by what I do. You believe that there is one God. good! Even the demons believe that - and shudder". (James 2:14-19)

James is arguing that faith (right beliefs or doctrine) can not be separated from works (obedient action). What we do ultimately reflects what we believe and who we are. Alec Motyer, in his commentary on *The Message of James,* says it like this, "James just says *works,* and into that one word he packs all that should be distinctive about the person who believes and is saved."[8]

Faith and works are related and inseparable. Just as a good spring provides good water and a good fruit tree provides good fruit in season, so real faith produces good works. Faith must be active. It is not good enough to have the "right" doctrine (although this is important). Right doctrine must lead us to actions that reflect the reality of this doctrine in real life. Remember that James said that the demons have right doctrine and shudder. They shudder because they have not acted on it and will one day be judged by its standard.

Hindrances to Hearing and Obeying God's Voice

The Bible says that hearing and obeying the voice of God is critical for our growth and effectiveness as Christians. If we are not hearing His voice on a regular basis, there might be something wrong. Granted, there are wilderness times when we do not hear God and must persevere, but these are exceptional times for most believers. Under most circumstances, we have access to God in two-way communication. When we are not hearing from Him, there are hindrances that need to be removed for us to be able to hear again.

Larry Lea, in his book *The Hearing Ear*, describes three major hindrances and two additional hindrances to our hearing. The three major hindrances which he calls "the big ones" include,

1. Unbelief - an unwillingness to trust God and His ability to come through on His promises.
2. An undeveloped spirit - a lack of sensitivity to the Spirit based in a dependence upon sight rather than faith.
3. A spirit of deafness - an inability to hear because of unforgiveness in our lives toward self, others, and/or God. Unforgiveness can provide Satan an inroad into our lives for "torment" (see Matthew 18:23-35).

The two additional hindrances that he mentions are,
4. A callused conscience - a lack of moral sensitivity because of sin and rationalization.
5. Neglect - an inability to hear because we are not spending time with God.[9]

There are probably other hindrances to our hearing the voice of God but these seem to be some of the major ones. If we are to learn how to hear and obey the voice of God on a regular and ongoing basis, we will want to explore these hindrances from a Biblical standpoint and find ways to remove them.

The other side of the hearing/obeying coin involves obedience. Learning to be obedient is a process. God will lead us through numerous situations and incidents which He uses to check our willingness to be obedient. We call these obedience checks. Obedience is a characteristic which needs to be established in our inner lives. It needs to become a natural response to God's leading. In the early years of ministry, God works to check a leader's willingness to obey. Leaders who learn to obey will be developed and released into more responsible positions of influence. At each new level of influence and leadership responsibility, God tests the leaders willingness to obey. What we hear from God might involve some difficult choices, personal vulnerability, or even some hardship.

Bobby Clinton lists seven different types of obedience checks that he has observed God use to check a leader's willingness to obey. These include,

1. A willingness to trust God about possessions and giving - God may ask us to tithe regularly and/or give sacrificially (see Malachi 3:6-12).
2. A willingness to trust God about choice of a mate and putting God first - God may ask us to wait on marriage or even to remain single so that His highest purpose can be realized in and through us (see Matthew 6:33 and Ephesians 5:21-33).
3. A willingness to trust God to use us in ministry - God may ask us to serve him in difficult and obscure circumstances (see Luke 16:10).
4. A willingness to trust a truth that God has shown - God may ask us to suffer for him in some way or to stand firm on the basis of something He has revealed to us. (see Matthew 5:10-12 and Philippians 3:10).
5. A willingness to forgive - God may check us to see if we are willing to extend forgiveness to others who have wronged us. He might allow us to suffer circumstantially or at the hands of others so that we can learn the freedom of forgiveness (see Matthew 18:21-22 and Luke 23:34).
6. A willingness to confess something - God may bring up unconfessed sin that needs to be dealt with if we are to go on with Him (see John 21:1-19).
7. A willingness to right a continuing wrong - God may ask us to make restitution for our sin against another (see Exodus 22:1, 12 and Matthew 5:23-24).[10]

In all of these types of obedience checks, there is great potential for growth. The challenge to obey God in some of these situations may cause us to feel fearful or insecure. Choosing to obey God in them will definitely lead to deeper intimacy and trust in Him. We will come out on the other side of the obedience check with a deeper understanding of God, ourselves and His purposes.

There are many hindrance to obedience. Obedience goes against our flesh and the dominant values of the world around us. Obedience is costly. It may cost us our pride, our possessions, or our popularity. To follow Christ means to take up our cross daily (see Luke 14:27). We must learn how to die to ourselves (see Romans 5:11-14), not to be conformed to the values of the world system (see Romans 12:1-2), and to put on the full armor of Christ (Ephesians 6:10-18). But why do we disobey? Usually it is because we are afraid.

Fear is the great enemy of faith and obedience. When it gets right down to it, our obedience depends on whether or not we trust or are willing to trust God's ability to do the best for us (by His definition). Fear can be a paralyzing reality but there is a greater reality that can free us from fear. The Bible says that "perfect love drives out fear..." (I John 4:18). What do we have to fear if we will embrace a God who has proven His love for us by allowing His Son to die for us that we might be forgiven of our sin and reconciled onto God!

God's love can break through the hindrances to hearing and obeying the voice of God, if we will let it. We can be "more than conquerors through Him who loved us" (Romans 8:37, also see Romans 8:38-39). We need to take courage, because "the one who is in you is greater than the one who is in the world" (I John 4:4). Jesus has overcome the world (see John 16:33). If we believe this, we will break the power of fear by obeying His voice. God out of His love will meet us.

Hearing and obeying the voice of God are inseparable parts of the dynamic love relationship that we can have with God and that will lead to our freedom and God's glory. Developing the abilities to hear and obey the voice of God are absolutely critical for us as we begin to reach out to others in ministry.

Faithfulness in the inner-life growth stage where we first develop relationship with God, integrity, and a capacity to hear and obey God form the foundation for success in ministry. The initial aspects of ministry maturing will be the topics of our next few chapters.

Evaluation and Application

1. Prayerfully ask God to lead you to the hearing and/or obedience aspect of this chapter that He would like you to focus on.

2. Reread that section or sections and look up all the supporting passages while asking God to reveal Himself and His purposes to you.

3. Write down your insights and ask God how He wants you to apply these insights.

4. Write down a strategy for applying these insights, act on them, and evaluate.

5. If you discover that you need to make restitution or seek reconciliation, ask God for a specific approach and prayerfully follow through.

---

[1] John Wimber and Kevin Springer, Power Points. San Francisco: HarperCollins, 1991, p. 19.

[2] James M. Boice, Foundations of the Christian Faith. Downers Grove, IL: Intervarsity Press, 1986, p. 30.

[3] Walter A. Elwell (editor), Encyclopedia of the Bible. Grand Rapids: Baker Book House, 1988, p. 18-45.

[4] Walter A. Elwell (editor), Topical Analysis of the Bible. Grand Rapids: Baker Book House, 1991, p. 158-160.

[5] Dick Eastman, Challenge the World School of Prayer Manual, Every Home For Christ, 1991, p. 159-167.

[6] Mark Virkler, Dialogue With God. Plainfield, NJ: Bridge Publishers, 1986, p. 5-7.

[7] Eastman, p. 167-170.

[8] Alec Motyer, The Message of James, Downers Grove, IL: Intervarsity Press, 1985, p.

[9] Larry Lea, The Hearing Ear, Altamonte Springs, FL: Creation House, 1988, see chapters 3-4.

[10] Clinton, Leadership Development Theory, p. 129.

6

Early Challenges in Ministry

I (Richard) entered the ministry at the ripe old age of 24. My entire focus in those first few years was on being successful in the ministry. I placed a heavy stress on getting results in ministry. I was a part of a church planting movement made up of young leaders. Our regional pastors meetings were filled with reports and stories about how big the church was and how many people were being touched by the ministry and whatever exciting thing that God had done last week in the church. Effectiveness in ministry was measured primarily by what we got done, by what we were achieving for God.

It was about two years into the ministry that I remember a prayer dialogue that I had with God. In this prayer time, God began to give me perspective on what He was doing in me and through me. I was struggling with what I believed were less than average "results" in the ministry. According to the church planting measurement standards of our group, I was supposed to have about 200 adults by this time. (There were only about 60.) Things were not progressing as fast as I wanted them to and I was frustrated. I felt that the lack of results was a direct evaluation of my worth in ministry and as a result, I was struggling with my own confidence and questioning my leadership and ministry abilities.

I decided to get away to an isolated place to pray and lay my thoughts and feelings out before God. I didn't write down the entire conversation that I had with God that day but I remember the gist of it. Here is how it went:

Me: "God, I am frustrated. Why aren't things happening? What am I doing wrong?"

God: "Things are going well."

Me: "How can you say that! The ministry obviously isn't successful."

God: "What do you mean by successful?"

Me: "Growth in numbers, conversions, demonstrations of Your power, financial stability, etc."

God: "What do you think would happen if I gave you what you wanted?"

Me: "I don't know but I think it would be great!"

God: "*You are not ready for success as you measure it.*"

Me: "What do you mean?"

God: "There are a number of things that you need to learn. There are things about Me that you need to learn. There are many lessons that you need to learn...lessons concerning the importance of godly character, lessons concerning how ministry to people is best delivered and structured, lessons concerning how authority works, lessons concerning how important relationships are, lessons concerning how to understand and communicate your values, and lessons about life. If I granted you success as you think of it, it would cause difficulty for many of your followers and might have severe ramifications on some. Richard, things are progressing at the right pace. You are learning valuable things these days. Learn to be content."

At this point during the prayer time, I grew very still and silent before God as He began to reveal what some of those ramifications might be if He granted me success as I viewed it. I remember thinking about other young leaders who seemed to have the success that I wanted but I had watched their lives and ministries blown apart because of the leader falling or some other problem. This prayer time was rather sobering for me. I was very grateful that God was beginning to give me the perspective that I needed.

God showed me that He was developing me. Ministry results were important but were not the priority during those early years. *I was learning how to be effective in ministry but more importantly I was being shaped by God into the kind of person and leader that He wanted me to be.*

Years of leadership research confirms that this is generally true for every leader. During the early years of ministry development, God will teach you how to be effective in ministry but His priority will be on developing you.

In the last two chapters, we have looked at the issue of character development. In this chapter, I will talk about three major areas of development that God uses to challenge us and develop us as leaders during the early years of ministry. The development of Godly character is still the major priority in terms of leadership development but these three areas are commonly used by God to both form our character as well as teach us to become effective in ministry.

I will briefly touch on a leader's social base, insights about authority and relational insights. My purpose is not to teach you everything we have learned about these issues but rather to introduce you to them so that you might be aware of them. As a result, when God initiates processing activity designed to shape you and teach you lessons in these areas, you will be aware of the issues.

A Leader's Social Base

A leader's social base refers to "the personal living environment out of which a leader operates and which provides emotional support, economic support, strategic support, and basic physical needs."[1]

More than ever before, we are recognizing how deeply a leader's social environment impacts how he/she operates in ministry. This impact is felt on many levels including the formation of values, behavioral patterns, and the way one thinks and responds to situations.

It used to be that society had fairly defined expectations and roles for people who were in ministry. This was especially true of leaders who were married. However, today we live in a time in which leaders are being challenged to face complicated social base issues. Families with any sense of Godly values seem to be disintegrating. Abuse of many varieties seems to be rampant. Social roles have undergone radical changes as they have been impacted by gender issues and the push for equality. In western society there is the tremendous focus on improving self and gaining personal control. Issues such as these and many others are deeply impacting leaders and their own social base situations.

Many young leaders do not pay enough attention to this area of development and pay a high price later in life. Many of the leaders that I have observed have been severely limited if not driven out of ministry because of problems related to their social base.

For example, I have seen several young couples who were involved in their first ministry experience. For a variety of reasons, one spouse was not in full agreement about being involved in the ministry. This created a lack of unity in the marriage. The tendency was for the spouse who was not "as committed" to feel abandoned and rejected which led to many instances where he/she sabotaged the ministry. On the other hand, the "fully committed" spouse tended to feel angry and bitter toward his/her spouse which created a bigger gap between them. In several situations, I have observed these unresolved issues lead to the destruction of ministry involvement or to the destruction of the marriage.

I know of another young leader who related his experience concerning his social base. In the situation, the husband operated from a fairly naive understanding of social base needs. He assumed that if he pursued God with everything he had, God would take care of everything. He either didn't recognize the importance of strengthening his social base or didn't know how to handle the problems as they began to emerge. Instead of getting help from an outside source, he pursued God and gave himself wholeheartedly to the ministry. The problems remained and eventually his wife felt neglected. His wife began to view the ministry as his mistress. How could she compete with God for his attention? This couple slowly grew apart and eventually ended in a painful divorce.

While this story is uniquely theirs, I have met many young emerging leaders who had the same approach to dealing with social base problems as the young man in that story. They pursue God with all they have but they either ignore the problems that emerge or, more commonly, they just don't know how to deal with them. They hope that because they are pursuing God's ministry, He will somehow deal with the problems.

I have also observed many single people who are challenged by their social base. Loneliness is a powerful enemy that every single person in ministry must face and deal with. Also, every single person needs to develop accountability in the way that he/she deals with finances, the way he/she spends their time, and how he/she deals with the physical drives and needs. I have seen many situations where a leader is sidetracked and taken out of ministry because of the social base problems that are related to singleness.

Whether a leader is single or married, he/she will need to have certain needs met by his/her social base. Simply having an awareness of the types of needs and challenges that are represented in this area gives you a head start as an emerging leader. It is our goal in this section to simply point out the various issues. Determining how you are going to work at solving the issues is up to you. [2]

It is important to recognize that we can do something about strengthening our social base. Being proactive and working to develop a strong social base to operate out of is one of the early challenges in ministry that each leader faces.

Over the various seasons of our life, different areas of need become heightened and need to be met. There are four basic areas of need: emotional support, economic support, strategic support, and social support as it relates to the basic physical needs.

> **Emotional Support**
> Emotional support involves such things as having companionship, someone to listen to you, someone to empathize with you and to understand you, someone who can recreate and relax with you and someone who can affirm you.

How is this need for emotional support being met? If it isn't being met, what can you do about it?   Questions like these are important to think about. For single workers in ministry, this area of emotional support is especially important. For newly married couples in ministry, it takes time and energy to learn to provide emotional support for one another.

> **Economic support**
> Every leader operates out of a financial base that covers living expenses, medical costs, educational costs and any other basic physical needs like food, clothing, transportation, recreational outlets, etc.

Finances can be one of the greatest areas of anxiety, frustration and tension for someone who is entering ministry. Whether a person is single or married, he/she must operate out of a financial base.   For married couples, it is becoming more and more common for both spouses to work. This reality causes all kinds of issues to be raised concerning the division of labor at home.

How are financial decisions made? What kind of financial standards and accountability are set up? Questions like these as well as others are important.

> **Strategic Support**
> Strategic support involves a deep level of sharing. It involves sharing our perspective about our ministry, career ideas, philosophy, problems that we face, our personal development. It involves sharing our dreams, visions and hopes about life and ministry. This perspective helps give meaning to life and affirms that what we are doing is important. The major choices in our life are influenced in this arena.

Who provides this level of sharing and support for you? I know many married couples in ministry who would answer that they provide this kind of support for each other. However, for some of these couples, it is not safe to discuss the core issues which involve giving our life meaning and purpose. This is especially true when it comes to sharing our dreams and visions about ministry and the future.

Over our lifetime, each one of us will go through various stages of development. In between the stages, during the times of transitions, we ask deep questions and assess our lives. The search for meaning and purpose, along with a need for affirmation, are important during these times. It is during these times that we need strategic support. Mentoring relationships are a primary means of getting this kind of support. We will address mentoring in a later chapter.

> ### Social support
> Social support is concerned with the basic necessities of life. How do we eat; where do we sleep; how do we wash our clothes; how do we satisfy our physical drives are all issues related to basic living.

Covering the basics of living takes time and energy. These needs must be satisfied. Whether the leader is single or married, he/she must work out these details. Dealing with our sexual drives fall within this area of need. Whether we are married or single, our sexual needs must be dealt with. I know of many married couples who have tremendous pressure and tension in their sexual relationship. Being married doesn't necessarily solve these problems. Being single and facing your sexual drives is complicated. Sexual desire and needs are not openly talked about in many Christian circles and people are left to work things out on their own. It is not within the scope of this chapter to address this issue except to point out that it is an important factor in establishing a healthy social base.

Over the first ten years of ministry, a wise leader will work to strengthen his/her social base in all four areas in order to avoid many of the pitfalls and problems that arise when a leader has a weak social base.   There are many seminars, materials and counselors available to help you understand the specific needs that you face.   Recognizing that we need to take steps to work on and strengthen our social base is the first step.

Insights About Authority

Authority has commonly been defined as the right to exercise influence over others. In the leadership context, authority is the right to exercise leadership influence over followers. This right is recognized by both the leader and the follower. In the Christian context, leadership authority is concerned with influence in the areas of morality, guidance for the group and providing clarification concerning God and His purposes.

Lessons concerning authority and its use are usually tough to learn for leaders who are just entering ministry. These lessons are usually high on God's training agenda for emerging leaders. Let me tell you a little story from my own history regarding lessons concerning authority.

I will never forget my first week of pastoral ministry. I had been chosen to take over a struggling church planting situation. The previous leader became frustrated with the situation and the problems. He found another ministry position without telling any of us who were involved in the church plant. Within a week of notifying us that he was leaving, he was gone. I was left in charge. I was the person delegated to lead the group.

Two days after being appointed the leader, I got a phone call from the worship leader of the group. He wanted to get together to talk over an issue. When we got together, he began the conversation with..."God told me that I am to be the pastor of this church...not you."   In my mind, I thought "Welcome to ministry, Richard." It took nearly two weeks of painful, agonizing meetings to resolve this initial challenge of my authority as the leader. I was willing to give this man the leadership of the group if that was what God wanted. In the end, God made it very clear who the leader was supposed to be. He used a variety of means to demonstrate that I was indeed God's choice to be the leader of the group. The worship leader recognized that he was not going to win in his attempt to gain control of the group left. He tried to inflict as much damage as he could before he left. I learned an awful lot about authority in those first two weeks of ministry. From that time to the present, I have been learning lessons about authority.

We live in a country and society which embraces and honors challenging authority. One of the legacies left behind by the generation of the '60's is rebellion against authority or questioning authority. Emerging leaders today have a basic mistrust of leaders who exert authority. In a way, I don't blame anyone for having a basic mistrust of leaders. Over the last 25 years, many leaders have abused authority and have discredited themselves and leadership itself. Leaders and leadership in our culture in this day and age have done little to warrant respect.

On a more personal level, people with authority or people in leadership positions have wounded and hurt others whom they were influencing. This is especially true of many broken and wounded family systems. In these settings, a basic mistrust of authority figures begins in the home as children try to deal with a parent who abuses his/her parental authority. Quite frankly, there are not very many good role models around. A leader who exercises authority in a responsible, honest fashion is difficult to find. Because of issues such as these, *God needs to teach emerging leaders to operate in authority in a Godly way.*

There are a number of lessons concerning authority that God initiates though a variety of circumstances, people and processes. The lessons concerning submission to authority are often the first ones to be learned. A basic premise in leadership development is this: *If you are going to operate in authority, you first need to learn to submit to authority.* If you have difficulty submitting to authority, you will certainly have trouble exercising authority in a Godly way. In American culture, submission has become a very negative word and submission to authority is often viewed as dangerous to many.

God loves submission. Learning to submit will teach us a lot about God, ourselves and others. God arranges circumstances and situations which will test your willingness to submit to authority. Submission is not easy to learn for many of us. In my own life, I have found that God put me in situations where I was tested in this arena in an interesting way. I'll tell you about one situation.

I got into a situation in which the leader of the group and I disagreed over how to raise up leaders in our ministry context. I felt that I was right. He felt that he was right. It was an issue of ministry philosophy. I went to the Lord in prayer. He told me to submit and watch Him work it out. This was hard for me to do because I felt that I was right. I submitted to God and the leader. This meant being quiet and supporting the leader as he operated the ministry according to his philosophy. Supporting his philosophy was difficult for me but I did it. As my wife constantly reminds me, keeping quiet is not one of my strengths, but I did it.

God did work it out. Eventually, God took the leader into another ministry and I was able to try all of my ideas about leadership development. We were able to maintain relationship and I know now that if I had pressed the issue, our relationship would have been strained and possibly severed. Interestingly, I found that I have been involved in many situations where I was the leader who was in the position of authority and a younger emerging leader challenged me on some issue. I chuckle to myself as I recognize God's shaping hand. Sometimes I ask them, "What are you learning about submission?" Submission is tough to learn but it is necessary if we are going to learn to operate in God's kingdom. Jesus submitted everything to His Father. We need to learn to submit everything to Him. God establishes authority structures and puts people in places of authority. They may not be perfect or "right" but God looks at our hearts and watches. Remember, *if you are going to operate in authority, you first need to learn to submit to authority*. Submitting to authority is all about trust. Do you trust God? How are you at submitting?

A second arena of lessons about authority concerns authority structures. As leaders, we operate in the context of established authority structures all the time. Every group has an established authority structure, whether is it explicitly known or not. In the situation where I faced a challenge to my leadership during the first two weeks, I was chosen to be the leader by the leaders of the church planting movement. I operated in the church planting situation with delegated authority at first. As I continued to minister to the people, I built relationship and began to operate in other types of authority, such as competent authority and spiritual authority. As leaders we need to learn to recognize the authority structures that we are a part of and learn the best (and God honoring) ways to exert leadership influence in these contexts.

A third area of lessons concern learning about the different types of authority and forms of power that support them.[3] There are a number of different kinds of authority such as coercive, induced, legitimate, competent and personal authority. (Spiritual authority is a type of personal authority.) Each of these types of authority requires some form of power behind them. A power base is the source of credibility or resource that a leader draws on to exert his/her influence. There are a number of different kinds of power that a leader might use. For example, force, manipulation or persuasion are all different power forms. In order to become effective leaders who operate in authority in a Godly manner, lessons need to be learned about authority and power and its use. It takes a great deal of time and energy to recognize the various dynamics that happen in any leadership situation. We don't learn these lessons immediately. We need to reflect on the issues of authority and the use of power. Are we operating in God-honoring ways?

A fourth area of lessons revolve around authority and conflict. In my early ministry, I was surprised to learn that God loves to use conflict to shape us as leaders. Many times the issues are related to submission, but there are other areas as well. For instance, how do you handle a situation in which a person challenges your authority? In the situation that I mentioned earlier, I learned a valuable lesson. My normal tendency when I am challenged or attacked in situations is to take it personally. Then, I attack the other person as my primary means of defense. I mentioned that God worked the situation out. Here is what happened. In this situation, God spoke very clearly to me and said, "Don't attack him!" I was to keep quiet and to let this situation run its course. God led me to just sit and wait. God resolved this authority issue by bringing to the light this leader's motives and his attempts to manipulate the situation to his advantage. The other people in the group clearly saw his motives and what he was trying to do. They rejected his attempts to take over the church. I didn't have to say or do anything in this situation.

Another type of conflict in which authority is a key issue is spiritual warfare. God's kingdom is at war with the enemy's kingdom. Conflict is inevitable. There is much to be learned in this arena. Leaders need to learn to recognize the strategies and plans of the enemy and need to learn to fight with the weapons that God enables us to use. Each believer needs to understand and walk in the authority that God gives to each one.

There are many lessons related to conflict which God initiates and leads a person through. I can honestly say that conflict has been one of the best and most consistent teachers that I have had. In the midst of conflict, I have learned a lot about myself, God and how to relate to other people.

The last area of lessons concerns the exercising of authority in a Godly way. As a leader is learning lessons about authority, the goal is to learn to operate in authority in a Godly way. Effective leaders move toward operating in spiritual authority as their primary power base. Other forms of authority and power may be legitimate but an effective and mature leader operates primarily out of spiritual authority. Followers accept and respond to the leadership influence of a leader who operates with spiritual authority because they perceive that the leader walks closely with God.

Spiritual authority is conferred on the leader by the followers. In other words, the followers recognize God's presence in the life of the leader and submit themselves to his/her leadership. Spiritual authority is gained as a result of the leader spending time with God, having deep experiences with God and having God demonstrate His power and presence in their lives. It is the deep experiences with God that form the basis of spiritual authority. Over the first 10 years of ministry, God will shape a leader by taking him/her through these deep experiences in order to deeply impact him/her. This process leads to the ability to operate in spiritual authority.

I believe that, in the early years of leadership development, it is crucial for leaders to gain insights about authority. I believe that this area of learning is even more crucial for the leaders who are emerging from the next generation. The leaders who are now in their teens and twenties have very few models of Godly leaders who operate in authority in a Godly way. Emerging leaders in this generation will have an especially difficult time learning about authority because of the lack of good models. But God is a great teacher. He will lead these leaders into situations where they can learn the importance of submission and the value of authority structures. God will teach them the importance of various forms of authority and power and the tremendous use of conflict to teach us invaluable lessons. Most important of all, God will teach them how to operate in authority in a God honoring way. They can become leaders who reflect God's love and mercy as they exert the influence that God has given them.

Insights About Relationships

Leadership influence happens within the context of people. Ministry is all about relationships with people. If you don't learn to build solid relationships with people that you are trying to lead, your leadership influence will be greatly limited. Relationships provide the context for leaders to operate in.

I'll never forget those early years of ministry. I was bombarded with relational issues. I was surprised to discover that a large majority of my time was spent in solving problems that arose concerning people relating with people. Miscommunications, hurt feelings, and misunderstandings were common. I had to learn to relate well with people...all different kinds of people. I learned to relate to people who agreed with me over some issue as well as people who didn't agree with me; people I liked to be around as well as people I didn't like to be around. I had to learn to love people, to motivate people, to inspire people; to listen to people; to help people. Ministry was all about relating to people. I remember thinking that my seminary training really hadn't prepared me very well for this aspect of ministry.

We, as leaders, never stop learning lessons concerning relating to people. However, during the first years of ministry, this area of development is particularly important and will represent a tremendous challenge. God intentionally shapes us and teaches us lessons in this area by putting us in situations where we are forced to learn how to relate to people as well as to learn the importance of relationships.

There are several different types of lessons concerning relationships that need to be learned. The first area of lessons concerns the foundational motivation behind our ministry. There are two things that the apostle Paul makes clear when he writes about spiritual gifts and ministry. (1 Corinthians 12 & Romans 12:1-8) First, love for God and love for others is to be the foundational motivation for the operation of our giftedness. Love is to be the primary motivation behind our efforts in ministry. Secondly, unity as it is reflected in relationship is crucial to the development of the church. We are to value diversity and uniqueness in each other. Yet, at the same time, we are to be unified in our worship of God and our fellowship with one another.

What motivates your involvement in ministry? There have been a number of times that God has challenged me in this area over the years. One of His favorite means of teaching me about love and relationship is to put me in a ministry situation where I have to learn to love someone who is difficult for me to love. These types of situations always challenge me to examine my motives in ministry as well as challenge me to learn lessons concerning relationships with people.

A second area of lessons revolves around learning to exert leadership influence with people. It takes time and experience to learn how you personally exert influence with people. We each have a unique personality, life experience and history which form patterns of behavior and beliefs about relationships. We need to learn about ourselves and others so that we can exert leadership influence in God honoring, healthy ways. We need to learn how to motivate people in healthy ways. We need to learn to inspire people and challenge them to grow. We need to learn to communicate or articulate vision and direction with people.

I grew up in a pretty conservative church environment. As I think back on my initial recollections and memories about church,

I now recognize that this church was pretty legalistic. In that context, I learned that guilt was a great motivator. Also, acceptance and affirmation were handed out on the basis of performance. The grace of God was mentioned but when it came to relating to God, guilt was used to make us respond in the "proper ways". When I began to minister to others and had to exert influence, guess what I began to do? Right! I also used guilt as a motivator. I found that it was easy to accept and affirm people who did what I wanted them to. God began to deal with me early in my ministry development. He began by breaking me and teaching me about His love and acceptance. To be honest, God is still teaching me how to exert influence in Godly ways. He is teaching me how to use love as a motivating influence. I am learning what it means to accept people as Christ accepts them. It is taking some time to change the way I view people and try to exert influence with them.

A third area of lessons revolves around relationship conflicts and problem solving. Building healthy relationships involves a number of complex factors. Trust needs to be earned and developed. Communication needs to be worked on. Listening skills need to be learned. Negotiating skills and attitudes regarding compromise need to be learned and put into practice. There is a tremendous amount of material available on the this subject so I won't go into any detail. God will teach us many lessons about resolving problems and conflict. His goal will always be to teach us what it means to love. Learning to love others in the midst of conflict and problems is a great challenge.

Summary

There is much more that could be said. However, I believe that we have shared enough to help you realize that these three challenges which every leader faces early in his/her ministry are crucial elements of your development. How are you responding in these areas?

In this chapter, I have tried to raise some issues. I have exposed you to three areas of development which represent early challenges that each leader faces in ministry. The three areas of development are common to each of us. Notice that each challenge involves an element of character formation. The lessons that we learn are unique. God leads us through situation after situation and person after person in order to shape us. Ultimately, we minister out of who we are. Our beingness is very important to God. He will work hard to mold us and shape us into His image.

Do you remember the prayer dialogue that I shared at the beginning of the chapter? It has been nearly 10 years since that took place. As I was writing this chapter, I have been reminded of many situations and people that God has used to teach me invaluable lessons about Himself, about myself and about other people. I thank God that He spoke to me so clearly so many years ago. I needed to change the way I measured and evaluated ministry success. I now would define success in ministry much differently. If God were to speak to me today, I wonder what that prayer dialogue would be about...

Lord, let's talk about what You've been teaching me recently....

Evaluation and Application

1. When you think about success in the ministry, what kinds of things come to mind?

2. Take just a minute to think about your own social base situation. Ask yourself the following questions: how are these needs being met? Am I just ignoring the potential problems or am I really dealing with the issues? What needs represent the ones that I am most vulnerable in? What can I do to strengthen my social base?

3. Think for a moment about the issue of authority. Ask yourself the following questions: When I think of authority and people in authority, do my thoughts tend to be negative or positive? In what ways have I learned to operate under authority or submit to authority? What

do I do in a conflict situation where I disagree with the person in authority over me? How do I treat people under me when they disagree with me? Who are the best leaders that I have seen in terms of operating in authority with integrity? What can I learn from their example?

4. Take a moment to think about relationship issues. Ask yourself the following questions: What are my biggest problems when it comes to building relationships with others? How do I handle conflict with others? In what ways have I seen healthy relationships impact a leader's effectiveness to influence people? How do I build bridges in relationship with people who are very different from myself?

---

[1] J. Robert Clinton, "Social Base Processing". Altadena, CA: Barnabas Publishing, 1993, 7.

[2] We would strongly urge you to get a copy of the "Social Base Processing" paper from Barnabas Publishers. You can write them at 2175 N. Holliston Ave.Altadena, CA 91001. This paper covers the issues in detail along with suggesting ways to strengthen your social base.

[3] For a detailed description of power forms and various types of authority, see Dennis Wrong, Power: Its Forms, Bases and Uses. San Franciso: Harper and Row Publishers, 1979.

7

Discovering and Developing in Your Giftedness

I (Richard) remember the first time that I seriously thought about my spiritual gifts. I was in the process of joining a new church. In the new members class, each person had to take a spiritual gifts test. We were given the test so that we could take it at home. We were to bring it back the next week where we would grade it in the class.

I remember that before taking the test, I wondered what spiritual gifts I had. The leader of the class had given us an orientation to the subject of spiritual gifts and had shared that each believer had a spiritual gift. This test was designed to help us discover our gift. He went on to share that the results of the test would be given to the various leaders of ministry in the church. They would contact us about getting involved in their ministry based on which gifts were discovered by the test.

Interestingly, I took the test alongside a close friend whom I knew pretty well. We talked about the test but didn't compare answers. After taking the test, I was not sure at all what the test would reveal. One thing was clear: most of the questions had to do with involvement in ministry in some capacity or other. I had not been very involved in ministry up to this point (I was 22 years old.) I remember being a little anxious about the results of the test.

The next week rolled around and we graded the test. The results of my test validated my fears and confirmed what I had suspected when I was taking the test...I had no spiritual gifts. The teacher of the class wasn't sure what to say as he glanced at my results. He just went on to look at my friend's test. Her results showed that she had 5 or 6 spiritual gifts with some 3 or 4 others close behind. I was amazed. I knew her pretty well. She had been involved in church life less than I had. How had she gotten so many gifts from God when I had been passed by? Over the next few weeks, my phone never rang. None of the leaders of the ministries in the church ever called me. On the other hand, for nearly a month, my friend was "recruited" by nearly every ministry in the church.

Now, some of you reading this story might think that I made it up. I didn't. This is a true story. For many people, this type of experience sums up their encounter with spiritual gifts.

How would you respond to this type of experience? Well, many people would just give up on spiritual gifts and just assume that they are not gifted people. Many people assume that God obviously chose to gift only the leaders in the church and some special people who could help them. Spiritual gifts are not given to everyone. Others might assume the test was not accurate. Others might wonder why two people who have nearly the same levels of ministry involvement could test so differently.

For me, this experience motivated me to find out answers. Since taking that test, I have set about exploring and learning as much as I can about the topic of spiritual gifts. I have been learning quite a bit. For example, I discovered that most spiritual gifts tests are based on ministry experience. If you don't have much experience, you won't test very high in any of the results. Also, tests results don't allow for ego strength. Ego strength determines how we answer the questions on the test. People with high ego strength will tend to answer "yes" to a question that is close to an experience they had once. A person will low ego strength will tend to answer "no". This explained the difference in the results between my friend and I. Also, the people who design these tests use their own definitions and understanding of how each gift functions to write the questions. I discovered that there are a wide variety of positions on how many spiritual gifts there are, the definitions of those spiritual gifts, which spiritual gifts are available to us today, and how to recognize a spiritual gift in action.

In this chapter, I am not going to teach on spiritual gifts. There are other resources that you can get for that.[1] *Instead, I want to challenge you to commit yourself as a leader to develop your own giftedness and through your leadership to create an environment where others can develop their giftedness.*

I have chosen to begin this chapter with this little story in order to point out the way in which many people are introduced to the topic of spiritual gifts. How were you first introduced to the topic?   Quite often, there is a lot of confusion concerning spiritual gifts and how they operate. The average emerging leader has to deal with this issue at some level both personally and in his/her ministry setting. At the same time, our leadership research points out that the issue of giftedness development is one of the top priorities of development during the first ten years of ministry. During the first ten years of ministry, the leader becomes aware of his/her own giftedness set and the need to develop it in order to be an effective leader.   It is the process of discovery and intentional development that I want to draw attention to in this chapter.

There are several key issues which need to be addressed in order for me to challenge you to intentionally develop your giftedness set. First, I will address the issue of accountability and stewardship which provide the foundation for my emphasis on development. Secondly, I will focus on the process of discovery itself. Thirdly, I will touch on the issue of intentional development.

The Issue of Stewardship and Accountability

You might have noticed that up to this point, I have vacillated between the use of the word "giftedness" and "spiritual gifts". There is a good reason for this. It has to do with two key issues: stewardship and accountability.

The Bible makes it quite clear that after we die, we will face judgment before God in heaven.   Read the following texts and let them sink in.

"For we must all appear before the judgment seat of Christ, that each one may receive what is due him/her for the things done while in the body, whether good or bad." **2 Corinthians 5:10**

"For this very reason, Christ died and returned to life so that he might be the Lord of both the dead and the living. You, then, why do you judge your brother? Or why do you look down on your brother? For we will all stand before God's judgment seat. It is written: As surely as I live, says the Lord, every knee will bow before me; every tongue will confess to God. So then, each of us will give an account of himself to God. Therefore, let us stop passing judgment on one another." **Romans 14:9-13a**

"Just as man is destined to die once, and after that to face judgment." **Hebrews 9:27**

"Obey your leaders and submit to their authority. They keep watch over you as men who must give an account. Obey them so that their work will be a joy, not a burden, for that would be of no advantage to you." **Hebrews 13:17**

Accountability is a scary word to many people these days. Accountability implies responsibility. Many people do not want to be held responsible for their actions. We here in western culture are pretty good at finding creative ways for releasing responsibility. However, when it is all said and done, we will be held responsible and we are going to answer *as individuals* before God. He will hold us accountable for how we lived here on earth. How does that make you feel?

It makes me feel two things...a little fear and a great sense of relief. I feel a little fear because I want to give a good accounting of my life. It is a healthy fear. It motivates me to live in a responsible way before God. I also feel a great sense of relief. In the end, God's justice and mercy will prevail. Every person will be judged. No one is going to "get away" with anything. This creates a sense of relief. It allows me to deal with the seeming injustice and frustration of living in a fallen, broken world.

How does this relate to giftedness? One of the things that we are going to give an account for is how we handled the resources which God gives to each one of us. Our personal giftedness is one of the key resources that God has entrusted to us. In order to see this aspect more clearly, we must look at the teaching of Jesus as it regards stewardship.

The Bible often uses human illustrations from a local context to help explain truth. Being a steward was a position that people understood during the Biblical times. It is found in both the Old and New Testaments. Eliezer is Abraham's steward. In Genesis 15:2 we learn that Eliezer will inherit all of Abraham's possessions because Abraham had no male children. The position of a steward carried a lot of responsibility. Years later, Eliezer is sent to select a bride for Isaac. (Genesis 24) It is probable that Joseph was the steward of Potiphar. It seems that the steward of a household had the oversight of all the affairs of his master, which included the care of his children as well as the master's property.

In the New Testament, the role of a steward was still a common position. In his parables, Jesus often used the image of a steward to communicate some important truth. Jesus often taught by using parables. Nearly 50% of His teaching comes to us in parabolic forms. A parable is a true to life narrative which teaches a central truth by using one or more comparisons.

We are going to look at two parables which have to do with accountability and stewardship because they form the biblical basis for my approach to giftedness development. In Matthew 25:14-30, we have the parable of the talents recorded. In Luke 19:12-27, Luke records the parable of the pounds or the gold coins.   At first glance they appear to be the same parable, but they are not. While there are some similarities, there are some key distinctions which give each parable a slightly different emphasis. Most of us are familiar with these two parables already. However, we feel that they deserve a closer look because together they provide a clear picture of accountability.

Remember that a parable is a true-to-life story which teaches a central truth by use of one or more comparisons. It is the central truth that we are after. The whole parable is given to illustrate that central truth with impact. To interpret a parable one carefully observes the observable elements: setting, story, sequel. Having done so, one can identify the comparisons between the story elements and the actual life setting. In a parable not all points in the story are comparisons. Some elements are needed to make the story complete. Once we have identified the central truth we can then explore its implications for application to other life settings as well as the Biblical context in which it occurred.

The Parable of the Talents: Matthew 25:14-30

Setting: This parable occurs in a series of interconnected parables which are explaining what Jesus' expectations were for His followers in the interim between His resurrection and His second coming. This parable is given to motivate the disciples to minister during the time before the second coming.

Story: The lord of the house was going to leave on a long trip. He left varying amounts of resources with 3 of his servants. One was left 5 talents, another 2 talents and another 1 talent. They were to manage his property until he returned from his trip. When he returned from his trip, he called the servants to settle accounts with him. The one with five talents had earned 5 more. He was blessed by his master. The one with two talents earned 2 more. He was blessed by his master. The third servant returned the one talent to his master. He didn't invest it for fear of losing it. He was rebuked by his master and thrown out.

Comparisons:

lord of the household	= Christ
leaving home on a trip	= Jesus going away to heaven
3 servants	= kingdom followers
5 talent servant	= person with large resources
2 talent servant	= person with less resources
1 talent servant	= person with relatively small resources
another country	= heaven or eternity
talents	= total resources: opportunity, abilities, gifts, influence, power, time, etc. That is, anything that a person has which can be used for the Kingdom.
coming back	= 2nd coming
settling accounts	= time of judgment or a time of accountability

Central truth:

You should recognize that you will be held accountable and rewarded on the basis of your service according to *your faithfulness* as it relates to your own gifts, abilities, and opportunities and you won't be held accountable in comparison with others.

Or another way to say it.

You wise kingdom followers must recognize your accountability for I will reward you at my second coming on the basis of service rendered according to your faithfulness to your gifts, abilities, and opportunities, and in terms of equal rewards for equal faithfulness.

Five Implications of this parable:
1) Don't compare your giftedness with others.
2) Don't be envious of someone else's giftedness.

3) Be faithful to what God has given you; God never expects
   out of us more than we are capable of doing.
4) The major basis of rewards is your faithfulness. Productivity
   is important but is secondary. If you are faithful in your
   efforts, you will normally be productive.
5) You will be held accountable for your giftedness and its
   development to maximum potential.

The Parable of the Gold Coins: Luke 19:1-27

Setting: The story of Zaccheus just precedes this parable. This
parable is given to correct the notion that the Kingdom of God
was going to appear immediately. Jesus was giving this parable
to encourage his hearers to work hard.

Story: There was a man of high rank who was going on a trip to
be made king and then he was going to return home. Before he
left he called ten of his servants in and gave them each a gold
coin. He instructed them to see what they could earn with it.
When he returned he settled accounts with the servants. Three
servants report to the king. One had earned 10 more gold coins,
one had earned 5 more gold coins and one returned the one
gold coin that he had been given. The first two servants were
blessed and given rewards over cities equal to what they had
earned. The third servant had his coin taken away and given to
the first servant. He was rebuked.

Comparisons:

Man of high standing	= Jesus
Citizens who detested him	= Jews who were rejecting Christ
Servants	= kingdom followers
gold coin	= service opportunities
king returning	= the second coming of Jesus
settling of accounts	= judgment or accountability

<u>Central truth:</u>

My kingdom is not coming right away. Do not lose heart in your service for I expect you to take advantage of opportunities to serve in the kingdom with zeal. I will reward you according to your zealous efforts and your results.

Implications of this parable:

1. All believers have the same chance to prove their zealousness.

2. Results in response to the ministry opportunities are important and will be evaluated.

3. We must use what we have to the very best of our ability.

Lessons concerning Accountability And Development

The parable of the talents stresses the concept of faithfulness. We are to be faithful with what God has given us. Each of us are given different abilities and gifts and are responsible to be faithful to what we have been given. If given more we should produce more. If given less we will produce less.

The parable of the gold coins stresses the concept of zealousness and results. Jesus expects us to take advantage of service opportunities, our abilities and gifts with a zealous attitude. We are accountable to produce tangible results before He returns.

When these parables are placed side by side, there is a certain tension that we must face in regards to accountability. On the one hand, we can take comfort that we will only be held accountable for what God has given us. He doesn't expect more out of us than we are capable of. On the other hand, the other parable stresses that fact that we are to push, learn and grow so that we can take advantage of every opportunity. We are not to be complacent. We are not to plateau in our growth. We will be held accountable to show tangible results in the ministry situation that God has given us. These two parables both point out different aspects of our accountability before God. We need to hold them in balance with one another.

At this point, you are beginning to understand why I want to challenge you to think about developing your giftedness in an intentional way. It is also becoming clear why I speak about developing giftedness rather than developing spiritual gifts.

Because of my understanding of accountability and stewardship, I talk about developing a person's giftedness set rather than just spiritual gifts. A person's giftedness set is made up of his/her natural abilities, acquired skills and spiritual gifts. I include all three elements because I believe that we are going to answer for everything that God has given us. He had endowed each one of us with certain natural abilities. Natural abilities refer to those capacities, skills, talents or aptitudes which are innate in a person and allow him/her to accomplish things. Acquired skills refer to those capacities, skills talents or aptitudes which have been learned by a person in order to allow him/her to accomplish something. Often, acquired skills enhance our natural abilities. God, through the Holy Spirit is the giver of spiritual gifts. It is the combination of these three elements that make up who we are in terms of giftedness.

Before we can talk about developing our giftedness, we must first talk about the process that is involved in the identification of our giftedness set. I have observed a common pattern that most leaders go through in order to discover their giftedness set.

The Process of Discovery

People primarily discover and identify their giftedness set by reflecting and evaluating their lives and their experience in ministry. Natural abilities and acquired skills can be discovered through reflection and self evaluation. Spiritual gifts are discovered in the context of ministry.

Bobby Clinton has identified what he calls the giftedness development pattern.[2] There are 9 stages of discovery and development. There are several terms that need to be defined before you will be able to understand the various stages. The gift-mix is a phrase which is used to describe the set of spiritual gifts a person repeatedly uses in ministry. The gift-cluster refers to a gift-mix which has a dominant gift which is supported harmoniously by other gifts and abilities.

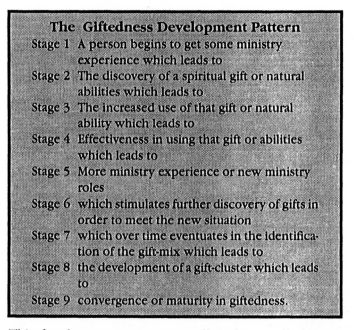

The Giftedness Development Pattern

Stage 1 A person begins to get some ministry experience which leads to

Stage 2 The discovery of a spiritual gift or natural abilities which leads to

Stage 3 The increased use of that gift or natural ability which leads to

Stage 4 Effectiveness in using that gift or abilities which leads to

Stage 5 More ministry experience or new ministry roles

Stage 6 which stimulates further discovery of gifts in order to meet the new situation

Stage 7 which over time eventuates in the identification of the gift-mix which leads to

Stage 8 the development of a gift-cluster which leads to

Stage 9 convergence or maturity in giftedness.

This development pattern actually refers to all elements of the giftedness set. The latter stages refer only to spiritual gifts since most natural abilities and acquired skills are discovered or obtained in the early stages of ministry. As one matures in giftedness, the emphasis primarily involves the development of spiritual gifts or skills that will enhance the operation of the spiritual gifts.

Here is how I diagram this process:

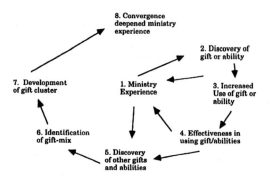

My Own Discovery Process

Let me illustrate this process of discovery with my own story. After taking the spiritual gifts test and discovering that I had no gifts, I became intrigued with the issue of spiritual gifts. I spoke to my father who had written a book on spiritual gifts. He shared with me that gifts tests were primarily based on ministry experience. The reason that I didn't have any gifts show up on the test was that I didn't have enough ministry experience. He really encouraged me to get involved in ministry at any level and that I would begin to discover what gifts God had given me through that process.

I followed his advice and began to get involved in ministry. At first, my involvement was simply participation in ministry activities such as Sunday school classes and small groups. I was also attending seminary classes at the time and was able to get involved in a number of ministry situations in the classroom. It was through those first experiences in ministry that I began to discover my giftedness set.

The first gift that I remember discovering was the word of knowledge gift. I was in a ministry environment where people were encouraged to ask God to speak to them and learn to give words of knowledge in ministry to others. The words of knowledge were primarily for ministry situations where I was learning to pray for healing. Over the course of a year, I found that I was constantly being used by God in this spiritual gift.

In the context of learning to pray for people, I discovered that I also operated in the gift of exhortation. I primarily exhorted people along the lines of encouragement and was not very strong in admonition or comfort. At the same time I was increasingly being pulled into leadership responsibilities in the groups that I was attending. I began to operate in the role of a pastor. Because I operated in the role of a pastor, I assumed that I had the gift of pastoring. As a pastor, I had the responsibility of teaching. Because I taught, I assumed again that I had the gift of teaching. I was involved in a church where we prayed for the sick regularly. God had used me in a number of situations where the people were healed by God. I would have put the gift of healing down as one of my gifts as well. Here is how I would have diagrammed my gifts.

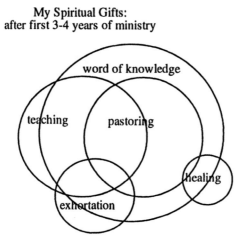

My Spiritual Gifts:
after first 3-4 years of ministry

word of knowledge

teaching   pastoring

healing

exhortation

A few years later, my father introduced me to the idea of a giftedness set and I began to see the bigger picture. I had strong natural abilities in leadership. I had always been chosen to lead things in school and especially in sports. Now that I was in ministry situations, I found that I frequently was asked to take leadership. I also recognized that I had strong natural abilities in creative and analytical thinking. I had the kind of mind that could see the bigger picture and break things down to smaller pieces through analysis to discover how it worked. Having done that I could find creative ways to put it back together and communicate it to others.

If you were to look at my giftedness diagram about 3 or 4 years into ministry, I would have listed the following gifts: word of knowledge (dominant gift), exhortation, teaching, pastoring, and healing. I would have listed my natural abilities as leadership abilities, communicational abilities (both written and verbal), and a creative, analytical mind. I'm not sure what I would have listed as my acquired skills but it probably would have been in the area of communication and counseling.

Over the last 6 years or so, there has been significant growth and development in my giftedness. My understanding of my natural abilities has basically stayed the same but I have discovered additional spiritual gifts and have worked to acquire skills that enhance my gifts and abilities.

In terms of spiritual gifts, there has been a sense of clarity that has come over the last few years. The first point of clarification that has come has been the difference between the gift of teaching and the gift of exhortation. I realized as I reflected on these gifts that I am primarily an exhorter. Teaching is a means of exhorting. I am not particularly gifted as a teacher but am gifted as an exhorter. Because of this I would not put teaching down as a spiritual gift. I would see teaching as an acquired skill which is part of learning to communicate effectively. Also, I discovered that the gift of healing was primarily attached to my role of pastoring and the environment that I was in at the time. I no longer see healing as a gift but rather see it as a Christian role that I participate in. There have been three gifts that have emerged over the last few years: distinguishing of spirits, prophecy and word of wisdom.   Each of these gifts are in various stages of development and were discovered as a result of repeated use in ministry situations.   At this point in time, I see my spiritual gifts like this:

My Spiritual Gifts: as I see them now

I have really worked hard over the last few years to acquire skills that would enhance the operation of my giftedness. For example, I have studied hard in the area of leadership in order to enhance my natural leadership abilities. This study has also enabled me to be more effective in both the word of knowledge and word of wisdom gifts as I interact with leaders. I have also gained analytical skills by learning various methods of research and by learning various frameworks which allow me to see the bigger picture in situations. I have also done quite a bit of work in the area of communicational skills. I have entered several mentoring relationships in which I have learned a great deal about effective communication.

I am not writing this story to exalt myself or brag about myself. I do not want you to get that impression. Rather, I have several major points that I want you to grasp by reading my own discovery process.

First, *giftedness is discovered over a period of time.* You can see by my own story that there is movement and discovery in the area of giftedness. Often, people take a spiritual gifts test and label themselves based on the results and fail to recognize that there is an element of discovery and growth.

Second, *it is possible to grow and develop in your giftedness.* You can see by my own example that I have intentionally worked at acquired skills and learning more about myself in order to become more effective in releasing my giftedness in ministry. I have also studied the spiritual gifts themselves and learned all that I could about the operation of them. This is an ongoing project of learning for me. Each year I design some learning goals and growth projects that enable me to explore and learn in certain areas. (Last year I worked on learning about the gift of prophecy. This year I am working on the issue of building faith.)

Third, *your giftedness set will change over time as you move in and out of ministry roles.* There are certain gifts that a person operates in no matter what ministry role he/she is in. However, in some situations, certain spiritual gifts will seem to "come and go" depending on the various roles that we have in ministry. In our leadership studies we have observed this phenomena time and time again. Bobby Clinton calls it the "role enablement pattern".[3] It seems that God will release certain gifts to people who need them in order to meet the needs of the situation. As long as the person is operating in that role, they operate in the gift. When he/she moves out of the role, he/she no longer operates in that gift.

The Issue of Development

The major thrust of this chapter concerning giftedness is on development. The development and growth in our giftedness set is critical to our leadership effectiveness. We minister to others out of our "beingness" or who we are. The better we understand who we are, the more effectively we can operate in our service to God. The issues of stewardship and accountability add special significance to the issue of development. We are going to give an accounting for all that God has given to us and how we developed and used it.

Development begins with the identification of our giftedness set which as we have shared, happens over a period of time. As we begin to discover our giftedness set, we can intentionally begin to develop ourselves. What is development in terms of giftedness?

When I talk about development in the context of giftedness, I mean moving toward maturity. By maturity, I mean that a person is operating in maximum potential as it relates to his/her giftedness set. Maximum potential is measured in several ways. First, a person operating in maturity in his/her giftedness does it in a Godly way. The character of God is revealed in all that is said and done. Secondly, the various elements of the giftedness set are operating in balance, harmony and synergistically. Each person's giftedness set is unique to him/her so maturity in this regard looks different for each person. Thirdly, a person operating in maturity in his/her giftedness bears appropriate fruit and is accomplishing the things that God has set out for him/her. *The process of development involves anything that helps move us along in any of these three areas.* I believe that we are to be proactive and deliberate in this pursuit.

The next question to be considered is: how can a person go about working on development? When a person looks at his/

her giftedness set, the question is: what can be developed? Can you develop a natural ability? In our opinion, no. It is not possible to develop a natural abilities. God sovereignly gives us our natural abilities. You can't sit down tomorrow and say, "I think I'll develop a natural ability!" You either have it or you don't. However, it is possible to discover some latent natural abilities and when you discover them it feels like you are developing it.

By definition, all acquired skills are developed and learned. Some acquired skills enhance our natural abilities. Some acquired skills enhance our spiritual gifts. This arena is an important one in terms of developing in our giftedness set.

Can you develop a spiritual gift? Many would say...no. We say...a qualified yes. We believe that you can develop (remember, moving toward maturity) in the area of spiritual gifts. Experience is a great teacher. This is especially true in regards to spiritual gifts and ministry experience. If a person is oriented to learning from experience, then he/she can learn a great deal about the use of spiritual gifts in ministry. Besides ministry experience, there is much to be learned by studying about the gifts themselves. There are numerous books on spiritual gifts which are helpful in understanding spiritual gifts and how people view them. The Scriptures are not completely clear about how many spiritual gifts there are and how they work or even what they are. As you read various spiritual gift materials, be aware that there is a wide range of opinion and beliefs about spiritual gifts. Lastly, it is definitely possible to acquire skills which enhance the use of spiritual gifts.

Summary

During the first 10 years of ministry, discovering and developing your giftedness set is a primary leadership task. Most leaders are not intentional about development. In fact, most leaders are not intentional about discovering their giftedness set either. At most, leaders may interact with the issue of spiritual gifts as an exercise in identification but never think about development. I have shared with you some Biblical and philosophical motivation to become intentional and deliberate in developing your giftedness set.

I have not tried to teach on the subject of giftedness but rather have focused on motivating you and making you aware of some key issues as it relates to giftedness. I would highly encourage you to follow up on this issue by getting the giftedness manual mentioned in the footnote earlier in the chapter. This manual will provide everything that you need to get started in identifying your giftedness set as well as providing some helpful insight about development.

Evaluation and Application

1. How do you respond to the issue of stewardship and accountability? Look at the two parables mentioned on this issue. How do you react to the teaching of Jesus? How do the implications of these texts impact you? Share your thoughts with a close friend.

2. What was your initial experience with spiritual gifts like? Have you ever tried to identify your spiritual gifts?

---

[1]My father and I just co-authored a self study manual on giftedness which covers what we have learned about spiritual gifts and leadership development. It is called Developing Leadership Giftedness and is available through Barnabas Publishers, 2175 N. Holliston Ave. Altadena, CA 91001.
[2]Clinton, Leadership Emergence Theory, p. 365.
[3]Clinton, (1989), p. 362.

8

Responding to God

Introduction

Up to this point we have commented on two important variables that are related to a leader's development: time and God's shaping activity. We have written about the need to view ministry and leadership development over a lifetime. Leadership development is a process that continues throughout our lives. We outlined six distinct phases of development. Each phase gives us perspective on the kinds of things that God is doing and how we are being shaped by Him. The time variable is crucial to understand because it allows us to view our own life and ministry with the bigger picture in mind.

We have also written about the processing variable. Processing involves God's shaping activity in our lives. God uses people, circumstances and various incidents to shape us, to mold us, to teach us valuable lessons about Him, ourselves and others. God uniquely shapes each individual so that he/she may accomplish the destiny that God has laid out for him/her.

In this chapter, I (Richard) am going to write about the third major variable in leadership development. Over our lifetime, God initiates processing or shaping activity which is designed to prepare us, train us and release us into effective service for Him. The third major variable in leadership development deals with our responses to God's shaping activity. How we respond to God's shaping activity over our lifetime makes a difference in our leadership development. In our leadership courses at Fuller, we call this the response premise.

> **The Response Premise**
> The time of development of a leader depends upon his/her response to processing. Rapid recognition and a positive response to God's processing speeds up development. Slower recognition or a negative response delays development.[1]

One of the major goals that Paul and I have in writing this book is for emerging leaders to gain clearer perspective on God's development of leaders over a lifetime. We have chosen to focus our attention on the leaders who are early in the process of being developed, that is, leaders who are in the first ten years of their ministry.

Perspective concerning God's plan for developing leaders which we are alluding to makes the single greatest difference in the area of responding to Him. Perspective will allow a person to make good choices. Better perspective will allow a person to make better choices. Perspective provides insight and leads to understanding. Here is the basic premise of this book: *If we have perspective concerning the kinds of things that God does to develop leaders, we can more quickly recognize what He is doing in a given situation and respond positively to Him.*

Let me tell you a little story about perspective. Last year my father and I had the privilege of teaching this material on leadership development to a group of pastors and leaders in the midwest. Most of these leaders were what we call mid-career Christian workers who have about 10 to 15 years ministry experience. As we shared the concepts related to time, processing and response, most of the leaders could easily recognize these variables in their own lives. We talked about perspective and the power of perspective.

There was one pastor who shared with us some of the difficult processing that God had been leading him through in the past few years. As we talked about perspective and how God used various types of situations to teach us lessons about Himself, ourselves and others, he began to see the hand of God involved in his difficult situation. He began to recognize some lessons that God was challenging him to learn.

We talked about how God uses difficult situations to process us in deep ways. We talked about the issue of response. *In a crisis situation (which he was in), you have two basic responses: you can go deep with God or you can turn from God.* We challenged him to go deep with God. He got excited about what he was learning because he could "see" the hand of God and was beginning to articulate what he was learning. He wasn't excited about the circumstances under which he was learning but he began to recognize God's involvement in the situation. This is the power of perspective.

In the context of listening to him share what he was learning, I made the comment that it seemed as though he was on a "fast track" in terms of learning deep lessons about God, himself and others. I challenged him to embrace the lessons and learn them well because I felt (in a prophetic sense) that something else was coming. I felt that a situation was coming where he would use what he was learning.

I didn't see or hear from this pastor for five months but I heard one report about him. Within about a month (I'm not sure exactly when), God took his daughter home to heaven. She had been fighting a disease for some time. In September, he had shared with all of us that God had spoken to him that God was going to use his daughter to bring glory to His name. He shared that he believed that God was going to heal his daughter. She died about a month later.

When I heard the report about his daughter, I remembered praying for the family and for this pastor. About three months later, I had the privilege of doing some ministry in the same area of the country again. When I arrived, I asked some of the people with whom I was staying with how the pastor and his family were doing. They responded that they were amazed at the pastor's response to the situation. They reported that he seemed so strong in the situation.

Later that night, I was speaking at a meeting. When I started to speak, I saw the pastor sitting in the back of the room. At the first break, he came up to talk to me. At first, he didn't say a word. He just hugged me and held on. Then he looked at me and said that God had used me (and my father) to change his life. I shared that I had heard about what happened. He told me that God had used me and my father in September to prepare him for what happened in his family. We gave him perspective about how God uses situations, like his daughter's death, to shape His leaders. God was shaping him. He said that on the day she died, he remembered something that we had said in September about responding to God in a crisis. He choose to go deep with God. He knows that God is with Him in the pain. God is providing strength for him. He is experiencing God's love in a new way.

At the end of our conversation, he said one thing that I'll never forget. He said, "God was right when He said that He was going to receive glory through my daughter. At the time that God told me that, I thought He was talking about healing my daughter. I didn't realize that God was talking about my response to Him in this situation. My choosing to embrace the pain and to embrace God (going deep with God) is the means God is using to receive glory. My response in this situation is speaking louder than any words I've ever preached about God." We embraced again and I was deeply moved.

This story is about the power of perspective. This precious pastor chose to embrace God and learn about Him. The situation that the pastor and his family are facing together is tragic and it hurts. He said that he (and his family) were still in the process of grieving her loss. We don't understand why God allows certain things to happen. But when we face crisis situations or difficult and challenging situations, we must respond. We can go deep into God or we can turn from Him. This chapter is about responding to God.

When God is developing leaders, He initiates shaping activities and gives us an opportunity to learn to respond to Him. *Godly responses to people, situations and circumstances need to be learned.* We, in our humanity, do not respond to situations in Godly ways. Our natural tendency is to respond out of our fleshly desires and motivations.

In this chapter, I am going to talk about three response patterns that God uses to help leaders learn to make good responses to His shaping activity. I will describe the ministry foundational pattern and two testing patterns. Learning to recognize these patterns in ministry will help you gain the kind of perspective that you need in order to recognize God's hand and respond to Him in a way that brings Him honor and glory.

The Ministry Foundational Pattern

Imagine walking into your local Christian bookstore and seeing a book entitled: "How to Develop A Successful Ministry— Guaranteed!" I wonder how many copies a book like this would sell. Would you be interested in knowing what this book has to say? I don't know whether a book like this is available or not. I afraid there probably is. At any rate, I am going to give you the secret to success in leadership development which in turn is the secret to success in developing a ministry.

I am going to describe a pattern God uses in His development of leaders that is rather simple, yet it has powerful ramifications. God develops leaders and ministries by using the following pattern. He never violates this pattern. It is so basic to development that I call it the foundational ministry pattern. Are you ready for it? Here it is:

> **The Foundational Ministry Pattern**
> This pattern describes a faithfulness/expansion cycle that occurs throughout a lifetime of ministry. Faithfulness in ministry tasks along with positive responses to testing lead to expanded ministry and a retesting of faithfulness at the new level.[2]

Jesus reveals an important principle that this pattern is based on in Luke 16:10. He is making some remarks following his parable concerning the unfaithful servant. He says in verse 10: "Whoever is faithful in small matters will be faithful in large ones; whoever is dishonest in small matters will be dishonest in large ones." *God honors faithfulness.* He begins the development of every person and leader by testing his/her faithfulness in small things. If you are faithful in small things, you will be faithful in bigger things. On the flip side, if you are unfaithful in small things, you will be unfaithful in bigger things.

Believe me when I say that you can take this principle to the bank! Believe in it and learn to recognize it. Think back over your own development as a leader. You will see this principle laced throughout your own development. How have you responded to the little things? Have you been faithful? What has your attitude been towards the little things? When you were faithful in a little thing, what happened? When you were unfaithful in a little thing, what happened? God honors faithfulness in the little things.

When God started me out in ministry, I was challenged to learn faithfulness. I was involved in a group that valued three things: worship leading, teaching, and ministering in power (mostly in healing). The first group that I got involved in had four people in it. There was the leader of the group and his wife who co-led the group. There was also a worship leader. And me. Initially, I was the only person in the group who was not in leadership. Can you imagine this group? I was the entire congregation. They watched me during the worship time to see how I was responding. The teaching was directed to me. During the prayer ministry time at the end, I was the only one to be ministered to. I thank God for that kind of beginning. It put me in a posture of receiving from God through others from the very beginning.

After the first month or so, the group began to grow. About three months into the group, there were about 10 or 12 people attending. It was around this time that God gave me a "faithfulness test". While I was hurrying to get ready to go to the group, I felt that God showed me a picture in my mind's eye of what He wanted to do during the ministry prayer time at the end of the meeting. In this little vision, I saw and heard what God was doing with the others and I saw myself leading this prayer time. It was very vivid. It was also one of the first times that I had every received a word picture from God like this. I got to the group a couple of minutes early and "interrupted" the prayer preparation time for the leaders of the group. I shared with them the picture that I had seen and what I thought it meant. I left out the part about me leading the ministry time. The leaders of the group encouraged this kind of participation from the group members so they weren't put off by what I shared.

At the end of the teaching time, the leader of the group shared a part of the word picture that I had shared with him and asked us to respond to God. We all tried to respond to God and waited for God to release the Holy Spirit's power. Nothing happened. Around this time, I snuck a quick glance at the leader who was looking right at me. Inside I thought, well so much for that idea. I felt a little embarrassed. Just at that point, I heard a voice inside my head say, "I asked you to lead this time, not the leader of the group." I knew at that point that I had to respond to this Voice. I broke the silence of the group and shared what I thought I had just heard. I shared that I felt a little unsure and insecure about what I was doing but I felt that I needed to take a risk and go for it. I lead the group in prayer and waited. God responded. Exactly what I had seen in the word picture happened. I was a little overwhelmed. That was my first faithfulness test in a leadership role in ministry. I have been facing faithfulness tests ever since.

If you are in a position of leadership that involves raising up and training emerging leaders, then I would suggest that you base your assignments of responsibility on this pattern. Faithfulness in little things should be tested. If an emerging leader is not willing to be faithful in the little things (with a good attitude), then I would be very hesitant to assign greater responsibilities no matter how "gifted" he/she was. Jesus used this principle in his training of the twelve. Look at how their development as leaders occurred. As they proved themselves faithful in the smaller things, Jesus released them to bigger areas of responsibility. They began with crowd control and travel plans and moved to winning crowds to Christ and leading the newly formed church.

Faithfulness is a great indicator of Godly character and God will test you in this area.   Over the first 10 years of your serving God, I would say that faithfulness is near the top of the list in terms of importance.   Learning to be faithful in the little things with a good attitude is critical to future development. If you don't learn this foundational lesson, you will plateau in your leadership development.   Faithfulness in the little things is the key to developing success in life and ministry.   Hmm, I wonder what the book in the bookstore says.

The Testing Patterns

As I have shared, perspective is the key to making good responses to God. Early in the development of a leader, God uses the concept of testing to teach us about responding to Him. The Scriptures are clear that God wants us to understand that trials or tests can be tremendous learning and growing experiences. (See James 1:2-4; 1 Peter 1:6-7) There are many positive benefits to going through them. Our faith is refined and purified and we learn to draw near to God. We will learn perseverance which will help us make it to the end.

There are two basic testing patterns. Both of them are used by God to teach us to recognize God's shaping hand.   The difference between the two patterns is simple. In one pattern, the person involved responds positively to God's test. This is called the positive testing pattern. In the second pattern, the person responds negatively to God's test which is called the negative testing pattern. I realize that these are not very creative names but they sure do describe what is happening.

God uses the idea of testing in order to check a person's responses to Him. In each testing situation, our character is being tested. Issues such as integrity, obedience, humility, honesty, and faithfulness are being tested.   Other types of testing involves God checking to see how a person responds to certain tasks or how a person handles responsibility.   In many of the testing situations, the person is not aware that he/she is being tested. It is our goal to help raise your awareness of God's activity so that you can recognize Him more quickly in situations and respond positively to Him.   Each testing pattern has three distinct aspects.

First, there is the test. Second, there is the response. Third, there are ramifications of that response.

> ### The Positive Testing Pattern
> The test -> a positive or Godly response -> expansion

The tests that God uses can come in every variety. God uses circumstances, people and incidents to test us in our character and our willingness to respond to Him. The key to responding positively in any testing situation is to recognize that in each testing situation, we have an opportunity to honor God. In order to respond positively, we also need to have a high view of God's sovereignty. If we believe that God is initiating or allowing the situation to unfold, then we can see His hand at work more quickly. God will use each situation to develop us if we allow Him to.

How do you know what is a God-honoring response? Because each testing situation is different and unique, we have to apply basic moral teaching from the Scriptures. No matter what the test is about, we need to respond with love, joy, peace, patience, kindness, goodness, faithfulness, humility and self-control. If we respond in these ways, we will learn to walk in integrity, honesty, and obedience. A response to any testing situation that is marked by the qualities mentioned above will honor God.

When a person responds positively or in a God-honoring way in a testing situation, God brings expansion to that person. The expansion can be a deepening of character or a greater level of leadership influence or more responsibility in ministry. Sometimes expansion is seen immediately but other times it is delayed.

A good illustration of the positive testing pattern is Joseph's story in Genesis 39, 40, and 41. The test came as a result of Potiphar's wife. She attempted to seduce Joseph. Joseph was tested in his character and in his behavior. Joseph responded in a God-honoring way. He saw that to give in to Potiphar's wife would be a sin against God. He turned and fled. He passed the test. The expansion is not seen immediately. Potiphar puts Joseph in jail. He spends two years in prison. It is not clear what Joseph must have been feeling and thinking during this time. However, God was at work. He used Joseph to interpret the dreams of the baker and the cupbearer in the prison. Eventually, this led to an opportunity to interpret a dream that Pharaoh had. Because of his interpretation of Pharaoh's dream, Joseph was promoted from inmate to the second highest ruler in Egypt. Now that is expansion! What would have happened to Joseph if he had given in to Potiphar's wife? I don't know. He responded positively in the situation. He maintained his integrity and God blessed him. If you choose to respond in God-honoring ways, God will bless you as well. He will bring expansion to you.

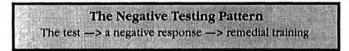

The Negative Testing Pattern
The test —> a negative response —> remedial training

In this pattern, the first aspect is the same. God uses circumstances, people and incidents to test us in our responses to Him. The second element marks the difference between the two testing patterns. In this pattern, the person either does not recognize the test as coming from God or chooses to respond against honoring God.

I have found that it is easy for a person to not recognize the testing situation as coming from the hand of God. It takes perspective and sensitivity to learn to recognize that God is involved in certain situations. This is especially true in situations where there are complicated and seemingly negative factors involved. Many people do not recognize that God loves to use tests in His development of individuals. This is especially true of leaders that He is developing. God uses tests to search out and reveal the true character of an individual. If we fail to understand this, we tend to respond to testing situations using our most common responses. That is, we will respond in our fleshly ways which are normally in opposition to God-honoring ways.

In the Scriptures, we see a situation in which the actual circumstances (in my opinion) are brutal. It occurs in Genesis 22 and it involves Abraham and his son Isaac. Every time I read this passage, I can't help reading it from a parent's point of view. We have the advantage of reading this story well after the incident was understood and interpreted for us. In verse 1, we learn that God was testing Abraham. It is important to note that Abraham did not hear a high pitched tone followed by the words..."for the next few days, we will be testing the emergency crisis responses of Abraham, I repeat this is only a test." What Abraham heard was God asking him to take his beloved son, the son of promise, the son whom he had waited so long for and sacrifice him on the mountain.

It took three days to get to the mountain that God had designated. Can you imagine what must have been going through Abraham's mind? Have you ever traveled for three days straight with your kids? I wonder if Isaac asked Abraham the same questions that kids ask today. Where are we going? When are we going to get there? When are we going to eat? I can only imagine that these three days seemed like the longest three days of Abraham's life.

What do you think it would feel like to tie up your son in order to kill him? Abraham did it. He was ready to fully obey what God had shown him. We read this story knowing what happened. God intervened and turned back Abraham's hand after seeing his response of faith. What a brutal test of Abraham's faith.

Do you think this little episode had any ramification on Abraham and Isaac's relationship? I can imagine Abraham a few months later asking Isaac, "I've got a couple of days off. What to go camping and fishing in the mountains?" Isaac responds, "That's OK Dad. Mom needs my help around the tent. Maybe next time." I really don't know what their relationships were like in those days but this incident teaches us something important about God. Faith is important to Him. Obedience is important to Him. God used this kind of test with Abraham. I believe that He might use trying and difficult circumstances to test other of His leaders. He might use something as trying and difficult to test us and our responses.

Sometimes the problem does not lie in the fact that the person does not recognize the test as coming from God but rather the issue is one of sinful rebellion. Sometimes, the leader recognizes the test and that he/she has a choice about how he/she is going to respond. For whatever reason, he/she chooses to respond in an ungodly way. Jonah, the prophet, is one of the examples that comes to mind. He knew what God was asking him to do. He choose to respond in disobedience initially.

Whether the person doesn't recognize the test or whether the person chooses to respond in an ungodly way, the result is the same. God enters them in remedial training. Remedial training simply means that God gives the person another test. The person gets another chance to respond. The test will probably not come exactly like it did before but it will revolve around the same issue.

Jonah's remedial training environment left a little to be desired. I can only imagine Jonah's initial response to his remedial training class. First of all, he was probably wondering if he were still alive. Have you ever wondered what it must feel like to be swallowed by a huge fish? Most people feel squeamish about touching the outside of a fish. When Jonah realized that he had somehow stayed alive, he began to pray. God responded and the fish spit Jonah up on the beach. Then, Jonah was retested. The test only had one question. "Jonah, will you go to Ninevah?" How quickly do you think Jonah responded?

Remedial training is a testimony to God's grace and His love for us. Many people have an image of God as a God who gives only one chance to respond. If you mess up, it's all over. The Scriptures don't reveal God to be this way. He wants us to learn to respond to Him in Godly ways because He wants to bless us. He wants to draw us close to Him and relate to us in intimate ways. He wants us to walk closely to Him so that we can enter into His love and be used in His Kingdom. He wants us to inherit all that He has for us.

If a person continues to respond negatively to God's testing situation, God will often move the person to the next level of remedial training...discipline. Hebrews 12:5-11 speaks of this discipline. It is discipline that is based in love. God desires for us to learn to walk with Him. The writer of Hebrews says that those who respond to the discipline will reap the peaceful reward of a righteous life. What a great promise!

However, I must also point out that God's grace and mercy do not go on forever for a person who continues to respond negatively. There is a point at which God turns away from a person who keeps choosing against God. With leaders, God seems to keep a shorter leash. Because of the influence that leaders have over people, God will not tolerate a set of ungodly responses.

This is especially true when the leader is aware of God's activity.

King Saul is an example of this. In 1 Samuel, we are told the painful story of Saul and his leadership. He was chosen and anointed by God. He was endorsed by the prophet of God, Samuel. The people of Israel rallied to his leadership and God gave him success in battle. However, Saul had some problems in his inner character. In 1 Samuel 14, we see the first hint of his impatience. He began to consult the Lord over the situation in the Philistine camp but quit before the Lord answered him because of the confusion and noise in the enemy's camp. This poor decision led to some other poor decisions. He marched his men into battle and they became weak with hunger because Saul made them take an oath that they wouldn't eat until the fighting was over. Jonathan didn't know about the curse and ate some honey. Later, the men of Israel sinned against God by violating some of the dietary laws. When Saul inquired of God for direction the next day, God didn't answer him and he knew there was sin in the camp. He made a statement that he would put the guilty person to death even if it was his son Jonathan. Jonathan admitted that he had eaten honey but Saul was talked out of killing him. This entire mess resulted from Saul's impatience and disobedience in getting God's direction. God entered Saul into remedial training by bringing him additional tests.

In 1 Samuel 15, God brings a little test to Saul. Samuel gives him the word of the Lord concerning the Amalekites. Saul is directed to kill and destroy everything. The warriors under Saul's leadership only destroyed the bad things but kept everything else that was good. This lack of obedience on Saul's part grieved God. Samuel went and found Saul and confronted him. Samuel pointed out his disobedience, which Saul lied about. Saul responded negatively to the test of God. God disciplined Saul by rejecting him as king over Israel. David was chosen as the next king. Eventually, the Lord withdrew completely from Saul and Saul went to ruin.

God does use situations to test us. Every leader can expect to be placed in situations that will test our responses to God. No one gets to bypass this learning environment. The key is to recognize God's involvement and respond in God honoring ways.

We control our responses by the choices that we make.

The Power of Choices

In our efforts to grow into maturity as people and as leaders, we must recognize on a daily basis that our choices and responses make a difference. In every situation, whether easy to understand or confusing, we can choose how to respond. God watches our responses to Him in each and every situation. Even in the most difficult of circumstances, He will bless our God-honoring responses by drawing us closer to Him.

I have found that life and ministry is filled with opportunities to respond. As time goes on, we can compare our responses to similar situations and measure our growth. I am greatly encouraged when I go through a situation and recognize that I am learning to respond in God-honoring ways as compared to a previous encounter. I can see growth and development in my life as I compare my responses to God, myself, and others in facing the situation.

A helpful paradigm that I use to help me recognize God's activity comes from my educational upbringing. I use the idea of pop quizzes, tests, and exams. Think about the situations, events and people that God uses to test us as pop quizzes, tests and exams.

I remember sitting in a classroom with a teacher who liked to give pop quizzes. A pop quiz is unannounced and is used by teachers to see whether or not the students are keeping up with their assignments. The pop quizzes generally are not difficult but rather test faithfulness to completing the assignments. I have been in classes where the teacher uses pop quizzes and have been in classes where the teacher does not use them. I can tell you that I prepared more carefully for the class that had the pop quizzes. I made sure that I had done the assignment and that I was ready. Now the teacher didn't give a pop quiz every class session so you were never sure if there was going to be a quiz or not.

Do you think that God gives little pop quizzes? God's pop quizzes are those little situations that He uses to see if we are learning and applying the things that He is teaching us. Have you ever noticed that as soon as you learn something that causes growth in you relationship with God, it is tested by a little pop quiz?   I believe that God loves to use pop quizzes because of the surprise element. We don't get a chance to prepare for the quiz. We have to respond to the issues out of what we have learned. Pop quizzes from God can happen at any time without any warning. I have found that God allows some little pop quizzes to emerge almost on a daily basis.

Beyond pop quizzes, God uses what I call tests. Tests are announced in advance and the test covers a larger amount of material than a pop quiz. Tests reveal at a deeper level whether or not some lesson has been learned. The Scriptures tell us that we will be tested in our Christian life. God brings tests into our life to see how well we have learned the lessons that He has been teaching us. As we develop in our lives and ministry, God will test us in certain areas for sure. For example, our faith will be tested. It is part of the refining process. Our character will be tested. It is part of the developmental process. You can count on being tested in your convictions about who God is and how He operates. These tests can come in all kinds of packages. God can use many different types of challenging circumstances to test us in these areas. Tests don't occur as frequently as pop quizzes.

The final level of testing is what I call the exam. An exam is given at the end of a section of material and is used to see if the learner has grasped the overall lessons given in the material. It is more comprehensive than a test.   Exams in our leadership development usually revolve around crisis events. In a crisis, what we are and what we really believe will come to the surface rather quickly. God allows and uses crisis situations to see how we will respond when the pressure is turned up. Exams usually only occur a few times over a lifetime.

God uses pop quizzes, tests and exams to see how we respond to Him in situations. He uses them to check on how we are doing. They provide us with a sense of evaluation and measurement in our growth.

What kind of student are you? I have found over the many years I have spent in school that I am a smart test taker. Maybe it's because I have taken so many quizzes, tests and exams over the years that I have learned to anticipate the kinds of questions that will be asked before I sit down to take the test. This allows me to prepare my answers ahead of time and I am not surprised when I begin to read the questions on the test.

This book is all about preparing ahead of time to answer the questions on the quizzes, tests, and exams that God uses in life to develop His leaders. Paul and I have attempted to give you some perspective about the kind of things that a leader needs to be learning in the first season of ministry. We can't tell you specifically what your questions on the pop quizzes, tests and exams are going to be. But we can tell you the general categories and the basic processes that God uses to develop mature leaders. This gives you an advantage. You can begin preparing your responses to the situations that God will bring you into.

I want to finish this chapter with a brief story concerning one of my heroes in the Bible. Daniel had a tough life. He was taken prisoner early in his life. He was taken from a life of nobility and made a servant. He was dragged out of his homeland and taken to a foreign environment. He would never again see his home and family. Talk about a tough break.

Yet in the midst of this, Daniel lived a life that honored God and he was greatly used by God. How did this happen? It began with a choice that Daniel made along with three of his friends. Somewhere along the route between Jerusalem and Babylon, Daniel and his friends made a choice that they were not going to defile themselves. They chose ahead of time how they would respond. In the first chapter, we see Daniel and his friends acting on their decision even though it meant that they could have been killed. We know the ending of the story and how God honored their decision by blessing them and granting them favor in the eyes of their masters.

Daniel and his friends knew before they got to Babylon that they were going to be tested in their beliefs and convictions about their faith and the practice of their faith. They anticipated the questions on the exam. They prepared their answers ahead of time. Throughout the book of Daniel, we see Daniel and his friends responding to situations that tested their resolve. The fiery furnace and the den of lions were not enough to turn them away from their decision. I ask you again, when did they make their decision?

We can learn from Daniel and his friends. We can learn to anticipate the kinds of situations around us that will test our faith, our character and our spiritual practices. We can make our choices ahead of time. When we find ourselves in the situation, we can act on a choice that we made beforehand. Now I realize that I am making it sound easier than it is. In real life, situations that we face are confusing and difficult to understand. However, it is still possible to make choices beforehand that we are going to honor God with our responses...no matter what happens!

Summary

In this chapter, I have written about the importance of responding in God-honoring ways. I have pointed out that we can choose in each situation how we want to respond. It doesn't matter how difficult or trying the circumstances are. We can honor God with our responses. I have pointed out the importance of recognizing two basic patterns: the ministry foundational pattern and the testing patterns.

If we can learn to sensitize ourselves to God's activity, we can learn to recognize more quickly what He is doing and respond in a God honoring way. God honors faithfulness in ministry. The ministry foundational pattern points out that God honors faithfulness in ministry by releasing the leader to more responsibility where he/she is tested for faithfulness again. Jesus pointed out that if a person is faithful in a little thing, he/she will be faithful in a bigger thing. At the same time, He points out the if a person is not faithful in the little things, he/she won't be faithful in the larger things.

God uses tests to see how we will respond to Him. If the person responds in a positive or God-honoring way, he/she will experience expansion in ministry. If the person responds in a negative way, he/she will experience remedial training. Positive responses will speed up development while negative responses slow development down or hinder it altogether.

The key to making good responses to God is recognizing each opportunity or situation as a chance to make a God-honoring choice. The power of making God-honoring choices is within our control. We may not be able to control circumstances and situations in our life but we can control how we respond to God in them. I encourage all of you to recognize the sovereign hand of God in each situation and to respond in a way that honors Him.

Evaluation and Application

1. Can you think of a situation in your life where the power of perspective was evident? Your perspective of the situation allowed you to "see the bigger picture" and respond accordingly. On the other hand, have there been situations in your life where you lacked perspective? What were these situations like?

2. How has God tested your faithfulness in the little things? How have you responded when you were asked to serve in ways that were not recognized or valued as highly as other areas of service? Share your answer with someone else.

3. Describe a testing situation that you know that God led you through in which you responded positively to Him. Describe the test, your response and identify the expansion that God brought as a result.

4. Describe a testing situation that you know that God led you through in which you responded negatively to Him. Describe the test, your response, and identify the remedial training that God brought as a result. When you were retested, how did you respond?

---

[1]Clinton, Leadership Emergence Theory, p. 359.
[2]Clinton, (1989), p. 359.

9

The Power of Mentoring

I (Paul) was visiting an evangelical seminary as a prospective student when an older man came out of an office and headed in my direction. When he came near to me he stuck out his hand and introduced himself as Vernon Grounds, the President of the seminary.

Although the seminary enrolled a couple of hundred students, he had recognized me as a visitor and took the time to introduce himself. He not only introduced himself but asked me to come into his office for a visit before I left campus that day. An appointment was set up and we spent about an hour getting to know one another.

Vernon was a very bright and well educated teacher and administrator who had given much of his life to the seminary because it afforded him an opportunity to invest his life in young men and women whom God was calling and equipping for the ministry of the gospel. He personally met with every student for at least one meal during their seminary career and always had a small group of young men who he met with on a regular basis to encourage and challenge.

At the conclusion of our meeting he offered to meet with me on a regular basis if I decided to attend the seminary. I did not finish my seminary training at this school but I spent two quarters there before transferring to another seminary to complete my studies. During my two quarters there Vernon was true to his commitment and I was forever changed.

Wednesday mornings at 6 three other students and I would meet in Vernon's office for muffins and an "informal" time to chat with this wise and seasoned veteran of ministry. He would listen, respond, and challenge us from time-to-time. His involvement in my life did not end with these meetings either. He would occasionally ask me to do work at his house, or drive him to a speaking engagement, or do special errands for him. All along he was carefully planting the seeds of encouragement, vision, and care.

I still remember the morning I found a message from him in my school mailbox asking me to stop by his office as soon as possible. When I arrived, he shared with me that he had taken a weekend retreat speaking engagement for single adults and that he wanted me to recruit and train small group leaders. I was excited about the possibility until he told me that the retreat was scheduled for the next weekend just five days away. I finally agreed to give it a try, not because I thought I could do it but because Vernon thought I could.

It was through surprises like this that I began to recognize some gifts and abilities for ministry beyond what I had already known. It was through surprises such as this that I began to get a glimpse of the power of personal influence that one life can have on another. Although I transferred to another seminary after two quarters and have never had the close working relationship with Vernon since, he is still a model, counselor , and close friend.

We occasionally cross paths. We continue to write and occasionally talk with one another on the phone. And through all the ups and downs of my life Vernon has always believed in me, prayed for me, and been available to me as he had opportunity. It is people like Vernon that can make a critical difference in a young person's life. They can empower others to believe in God through the influence of their own faithful lives.

We all need people like Vernon in our lives. They encourage, challenge, and help us on our way to maturity in our faith and effectiveness in ministry. People like Vernon are called mentors.

Mentors are people who "empower another by sharing God-given resources."[1] Clinton and Stanley describe mentoring as "a relational process in which someone who knows something, the mentor, transfers that something (the power resource such as wisdom, advice, information, emotional support, protection, linking to resources, career guidance, status) to someone else, the mentoree, at a sensitive time so that it impacts development."[2]

Mentoring is a critical aspect of how God helps prepare young men and women for effective lives and ministry. Moses mentored Joshua (see Numbers 11:28 and 27:18-21), Elijah mentored Elisha (see I Kings 19:19-21 and II Kings 2:1-18), Barnabas mentored Paul (see Acts 9:27, 11:25-25, and 13:1-2), Paul mentored Timothy and Titus (see Acts 16:1-5 and I & II Timothy and Titus), and the greatest example of mentoring is Jesus with his disciples.

Jesus could command great numbers of people through His teaching and healing ministry (see Matthew 4:23-25) but He chose to invest much of His time and energy in the lives of a few (see Mark 1:16-18; 3:13-19, 4:33-34). A. B. Bruce in his classic study of Jesus' discipleship technique entitled *The Training of the Twelve* says,

> "The twelve arrived at their final intimate relation to Jesus only by degrees, three stages in the history of their fellowship with Him begging distinguishable. In the first stage they were simply believers in Him as the Christ, and His occasional companions at convenient, particular festive, seasons... In the second stage, fellowship with Christ assumed the form of an uninterrupted attendance on His person... The twelve entered on the last and highest stage of discipleship when they were chosen by their Master from the mass of His followers, and formed into a select band, to be trained for the great work of the apostleship."[3]

Jesus, of course, is the great Mentor. He is the example and source of all that we need to become like Him. But mentoring is also a training strategy that He used to impact the lives of those He chose to be with Him, to become like Him, and to carry on after Him. Ron Lee Davis calls this training strategy of Jesus the "mentoring principle" by which "more [quality] time spent with fewer people equals greater lasting impact for God."[4] The impact of one life empowering another results in support, accountability, maturity and effectiveness in ministry.

The Dynamics of Mentoring

Mentoring becomes more effective when we deliberately pursue it. Bobby Clinton describes effective mentoring as involving five identifiable dynamics: attraction, relationship, responsiveness, accountability, and empowerment (see Figure 9-1 - Dynamics of Mentoring Relationships).[5]

Figure 9-1 - Dynamics of Mentoring Relationships

Attraction which leads to **Relationship**
Responsiveness creates
Accountability which enhances **Empowerment**

Attraction is the starting point for any mentoring relationship. A mentor is attracted to a potential mentoree because of "leadership potential." A potential mentoree is attracted to a mentor because of his ability to teach the Bible, lead an organization, or counsel hurting people.

Out of attraction a relationship can begin. This relationship can become very involved, occasional, or passive depending upon the mentor and mentoree's gifts, abilities, philosophy of ministry, and/or schedule. As a general rule, the deeper the relationship, the more effective and deeper the empowerment that is received.

The relationship provides the chance for responsiveness. Responsiveness involves the degree to which the mentoree responds to the mentor's help. The higher the degree of responsiveness, the greater the chance for empowerment. A submissive, open, and receiving attitude on the part of the mentoree increases the speed and intensity of the empowering process in mentoring.

This next dynamic is called accountability. Accountability is ultimately the mentor's responsibility while submission is the responsibility of the mentoree. Accountability is not blind obedience but submission to the authority of a mature Christian within the context of the clear teaching of the Bible.

Accountability involves responsibility. It is holding someone responsible.

These four dynamics lead to an empowering of the mentoree by the mentor. Empowering involves insights, break-throughs, contacts, resources, experiences, promotions, etc. The mentoree is significantly changed for the positive by having been involved with the mentor.

When people think about mentoring, they often have in mind that a mentor is a special person who can meet all of their needs. It becomes apparent rather quickly that there are not enough of these "super mentors" to go around. This leads to the person being discouraged and assuming that there is no one available to mentor them. I have some good news for you. There are plenty of mentors to go around. But it will take a little hard work on your part to get the mentoring relationships going. You may have to provide some of the five dynamics that are mentioned above in order to get the mentoring help that you need.

For example, you may not be able to establish a personal relationship with a person who is an excellent teacher but you can provide the attraction, the responsiveness, and accountability. These dynamics will create an environment where you can be empowered through the teacher's insights.

One of the most helpful things to do in trying to get mentoring help is to identify your mentoring needs as specifically as you can. Then you can try to find a person or a resource that can help you meet that need. In other words, don't look for the one ideal "super mentor" who can meet every need. Find many mentors who can help you meet the various needs that arise.

Different Mentoring Types

Not all mentors function in the same way. There are different types or styles of mentoring. Clinton (1990) has identified nine types of mentors. The nine types fit into one of three grouping depending on the degree of intensity and structure of the relationship (see Figure 9-2 - Mentor Types and Relational groupings). The nine types include the discipler, the spiritual guide, the counselor, the sponsor, the teacher, the coach, the contemporary model, the Biblical and historical model, and the divine contact.[6]

Figure 9-2 - Different Mentor Types

Intensive	Occasional	Passive
|——————| |——————| |——————|

Deeper level of Relationship   Little or no Relationship

1. Discipler	4. Counselor	7. Contemporary Model
2. Spiritual Guide	5. Teacher	8. Biblical & Historical Model
3. Coach	6. Sponsor	9. Divine Contact

The **discipler** is probably the most well known type of mentoring. The primary thrust of the discipler is to enable the mentoree in the basics of following Christ. The discipler is usually very involved and deliberate in his relationship with the mentoree. Stanley and Clinton define the discipler as "a relational process in which a more experienced follower of Christ shares with a newer believer the commitment, understanding, and basic skills necessary to know and obey Jesus Christ as Lord."[7]

Many churches and para-church organizations have discipleship programs to train young believers in the basics of the Christian life. One example involves a church based program based on the "Timothy Principle." This structured program involves one obedient Christian empowering a younger Christian or small group of Christians to be obedient in the four areas of prayer, the Word, fellowship, and witnessing.[8]

Another example involves a para-church missions organization that runs residential discipleship training programs. These programs involve three months of training in the areas of hearing and obeying God's voice, openness and brokenness, intercessory prayer, and evangelism followed by a time of team outreach (often cross-cultural) in service, training, and evangelism.[9]

The second type of mentor is called the **spiritual guide**. The primary trust of the spiritual guide is providing perspective and accountability for the mentoree in the area of spiritual growth.

Stanley and Clinton define the spiritual guide as "a Godly, mature follower of Christ who shares knowledge, skills, and basic philosophy of what it means to increasingly realize Christlikeness in all areas of life."[10]

Richard Foster in his book *Celebration of Discipline* reminds us that legalistic compliance to the spiritual disciplines is not the purpose of the spirituality. Transformation in Christ from the inside out is the purpose and the disciplines can be an important means to this end. Foster says,

> "The Spiritual Disciplines are intended for our good. They are meant to bring the abundance of God into our lives. It is possible, however, to turn them into another set of soul-killing laws. Law-bound Disciplines breathe death. Jesus teaches that we must go beyond the righteousness of the Scribes and Pharisees (Matthew 5:20). Yet we need to see that their righteousness was no small thing. They were committed to following God in a way that many of us are not prepared to do. One factor, however, was always central to their righteousness: *externalism*. Their righteousness consisted in control over externals... The extent to which we have gone beyond the righteousness of the scribes and Pharisees is seen in how much our lives demonstrate the internal work of God upon our heart. To be sure, this will have external results, but the work will be internal."[11]

Spirituality mentors usually are most effective in helping believers who have already been discipled. That is, they have the basic practices of the faith established in their life. The person who needs a spiritual guide is someone who has hit a plateau in his/her spiritual growth and needs someone to come along and give him/her perspective on how to go deeper with God.

The third type of mentor is the **coach**. The primary thrust of the coach is to motivate the mentoree and help him/her develop gifts, abilities, and skills for effective ministry. Stanley and Clinton define coaching as "a relational process in which the mentor, who knows how to do something well, imparts those skills to a mentoree who wants to learn them."[12]

We see this type of mentoring in Jesus' ministry when He sends out the twelve (Matthew 10 and Luke 9) and the seventy-two (Luke 10). First, He taught them about life and ministry (Matthew 5-7). Next He demonstrated it for them (Matthew 8-9), and then he sends them out to do it themselves (Matthew 10). After the twelve return, He spent time with them in evaluation and further preparation (see Luke 9: 10-17). This pattern of training is central to Jesus' training ministry and that of such early church leaders as Barnabas and Paul.

Successful coaches are able to bring the best out in their teams when it really counts. Alan Loy McGinnis, in his book *Bringing Out the Best in People,* lists twelve rules that leaders use in bringing out the best in people. He lists them as follows:

1. Expect the best from the people you lead.
2. Make a thorough study of the other person's needs.
3. Establish high standards for excellence.
4. Create an environment where failure is not fatal.
5. If they are going anywhere near where you want to go, climb on others people's bandwagons.
6. Employ methods to encourage success.
7. Recognize and applaud achievement.
8. Employ a mixture of positive and negative reinforcement.
9. Appeal sparingly to the competitive urge.
10. Place a premium on collaboration.
11. Build into the group an allowance for storms.
12. Take steps to keep your own motivation high.[13]

These are the things that successful mentor coaches do to motivate and empower their team members for success. Mentorees find themselves in a relationship where they are able to experiment, grow, and prosper.

The fourth type of mentor is the **counselor**. The primary thrust of the counselor is to provide timely advise and correct perspective on viewing self, others, and ministry. Stanley and Clinton describe eight "empowerment functions" of the mentor as counselor. These include encouragement , being a sounding board, assisting in major evaluations, gaining needed perspective, providing specific advise, linking to informational and/or people resources, assisting in major guidance, and aiding in inner healing.[14]

A good counselor possesses the ability to care, listen, and provide needed resources when appropriate. Larry Crabb, in his book *Effective Biblical Counseling*, States that "it is our [believers who counsel others] responsibility as fellow members of the body [church] to continually remind and exhort each other to keep in view the goal of all true counseling: *to free people to better worship and serve God* by helping them to become more like the Lord. In a word, the goal is maturity."[15]

An example of the counselor type of mentoring in the Bible is Jethro with Moses (Exodus 18). Moses was faced with the incredible responsibility of leading and "judging" the people of Israel on their exodus from Egypt to the Promised Land. Early on in the exodus Moses received a visit from his father-in-law Jethro (verses 5-8). After a day of reunion Moses got back to his usual responsibilities of "judging" the people from morning until evening (verse 13). When Jethro saw this he became concerned (verse 14 and 17-18) and asked Moses about it (verses 15-16). As a result of their conversation, Jethro advised Moses to delegate the lesser disputes to qualified "under judges" and for him to hear only the most difficult disputes that could not be resolved by the "under judges" (verses 19-23). Moses took his father-in-laws counsel (verse 24) and implemented it (verses 25-26).

Wise counselors can be of tremendous help to us as we face the difficulty and complexity of everyday life and ministry. The Bible encourages us to seek out and to take seriously the counsel of more mature Christians (see Proverbs 11:14, 12:15, 15:22, 19:20). In times of stress we often need perspective that can come from a wise and loving counselor.

The fifth type of mentor is the **teacher**. The primary thrust of the teacher is to motivate through the importation of Biblical knowledge and understanding on a particular subject or issue. Stanley and Clinton describe the teacher as functioning in the following ways,

1. They know what resources are needed and available or who/where to approach/go in order to find out.

2. They know how to link mentorees to resources.
3. They know how to organize and impart knowledge to mentorees.
4. They know how to show the relevance of information to the mentoree's situation.
5. They know how to help mentorees to gain proper per spective for assessment and evaluation.
6. They know how to motivate mentorees to continue to learn.[16]

Motivational teachers are such a joy to learn under. They seem to know how to communicate truth so that it is informative, relevant, and practical. Howard Hendricks is an example of a teacher mentor. He has influenced a generation of church leaders through his teaching, conference ministry, and writing. In his book entitled *Teaching to Change Lives* he states that "teaching that impacts is not head to head, but heart to heart."[17] This type of teaching involves the three components of character, compassion, and content. Hendricks states that,

"For the teacher's *character* is what produces the learner's confidence... Second, it's your *compassion* that produces the learner's *motivation*... Third, it's your *content* that produces the learner's *perception*."[18]

Obviously, Jesus is the greatest example of the teacher mentor. He possessed all three of these components and the people "were amazed at his teaching, because he taught as one who had authority, and not as their teachers of the law" (Matthew 7:28-29). There was authority in the teaching of Jesus that was not present in the learned teaching of the religious teachers. They had content but often lacked character and compassion (see Matthew 23).

The sixth type of mentor is the **sponsor**. The primary thrust of the sponsor is to help prepare, protect, and promote a mentoree into a wider realm of responsibility and influence. Stanley and Clinton describe six steps that are involved in sponsoring. These include selection of potential leaders, encouragement, the impartation of skills, the linking of resources (education, training, finances, personal contacts), perspective, and inspiration.[19]

The concept of sponsoring was made popular through the works of Robert Greenleaf (*Servant Leadership*) and Tom Peters (*In Search of Excellence*). In both of these books the authors described some of the benefits of sponsoring or "championing" up-and-coming talent in the business world. Ted Engstrom, in his book entitled *The Fine Art of Mentoring*, has addressed this concept and its potential impact upon the church and Christian organizations. He says that "mentors worth their title will show a protégé how to work while others waste time, how to study while others procrastinate, and how to pray while others play."[20]

This kind of mentoring enables younger emerging leaders to develop their potential and begin to take their place as the mantel of responsibility is passed on to the next generation. The sponsoring of Joshua by Moses (see Deuteronomy 34:5-9), of Elisha by Elijah (see II Kings 2:11-15), of Paul by Barnabas (see Acts 9:27 and 11:25-26), and Timothy by Paul (see II Timothy 4:1-8) are good examples of the transition of responsibility from one to another and from one generation to the next.

The seventh type of mentor is the *contemporary model*. The primary thrust of the contemporary model is to be an example that others desire to follow. Stanley and Clinton describe the contemporary model as "a living person whose life or ministry is used as an example to indirectly impart skills, principles, and values that empower another person."[21]

There could be any number of examples of the contemporary model in the Bible, church history, or today. The patriarchs influenced their generation, the prophets, theirs, the apostles influenced a whole new course for God's people in their generation, the early church fathers established the form and doctrine of the church in theirs, the desert fathers influenced their generation in the areas of spirituality, the reformers brought the Bible back to the people of their generation, the revivalists brought life back into the state churches of their day, and today evangelists, pastors, and Christian leaders are influencing their generation. Each generation has contemporary models that provide an example that empowers others to be more like Christ.

Even though we may never have any direct personal involvement in their lives, they influence us. We are influenced by their public ministry, their writing, their leadership, and/or their life circumstances. Because their lives are usually public, we are exposed to them through others views of them in magazine articles, television interviews, and/or biographies.

Billy Graham is probably the best example of a contemporary model (at least in the west). He has served the Lord faithfully with his team for many years. He has preached the gospel all over the world to millions of people. He has been a source of encouragement to many. When he has failed he has been open about it and taken steps to remedy his failures. He seems to be finishing well.

One of the greatest difficulties that contemporary models have is that they are human and have limitations that might be overlooked or underplayed by enthusiastic followers. Some contemporary models take on the status of pop "idols" and when they fail to live up to the expectations of their followers there is confusion, hurt, and disillusionment. Contemporary models are people, not God, and we need to be careful that we do not "idolize" them to the detriment of our fellowship with Christ. Their lives should encourage us to want to know God better and to serve Him more effectively.

The eighth type of mentor is the **Biblical and historical model**. The primary thrust of the Biblical and historical model is to model a dynamic life of character, faith, and effectiveness that influences others after the model's death. Stanley and Clinton describe the Biblical and historical model as "a person now dead whose life or ministry is written in a(n) (auto)biographical form and is used as an example to indirectly impart values, principles, and skills that empower another person."[22]

There are Biblical and historical mentors who, through their lives and writings as well as others writing about them, can be of tremendous help to us as Christians and leaders. I (Paul) have undergone an extensive study of Biblical characters over the past several years using Clinton's leadership emergence model to survey the character's life and leadership lessons. Studies such as these can be tremendously valuable. The Bible tells us that we can learn from the lives of those who have lived faithful lives in the past (see Hebrews 13:7-8).

The last type of mentor is the **divine contact**. The primary thrust of the divine contact is timely guidance and/or discernment through divine intervention. This intervention can be "natural" and/or "supernatural."

The conversion and healing of Saul/Paul is an example of this (Acts 9). While on his way to Damascus to imprison any belonging to "the Way" (verses 1-2), Paul was divinely contacted by Jesus (verses 3-5). During this encounter he was blinded and told to go into the city of Damascus where he would be told what to do (verses 6-8). This is an example of "supernatural" divine contact.

Paul spent three days in Damascus fasting and praying (verses 9 and 11). during this time, the Lord appeared to a disciple named Ananias in a vision (verse 10) and told him to visit Paul (verses 11-12 and 15-16). When Ananias visited Paul, he prayed for his healing and filling with the Holy Spirit (verses 17-18). This is an example of "natural" divine contact.

Although divine contacts are fairly rare in most of our lives, God has used this form of mentoring throughout the Bible and church history at critical times in the lives of his people.

Ranges of Mentoring

Not every mentor is gifted in or uses all of these styles. Most will focus on one or several of these styles depending on their spiritual gifts, personality, calling, experience, etc. All of us do not need mentoring in all of these areas all of the time. Most of us will have a series of mentor relationships throughout our lives that will address special needs as they arise.

Mentoring on an ongoing basis seems to be important in the lives of growing, effective people. Stanley and Clinton have developed a constellation model to help us understand the range of mentoring needed in our lives (see figure 9-3 - Constellation Model of Mentoring). This model involves "upward mentoring" with someone more mature than us, "lateral or peer mentoring" with peers who are involved in similar situations and peers who are involved in different situations, and "downward mentoring" with emerging younger Christians.[23]

Figure 9-3 - Constellation Model of Mentoring

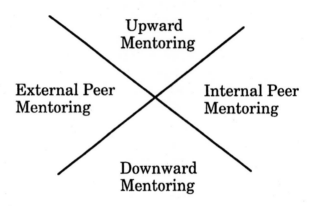

Each of these different kinds of mentoring relationships are important to help provide us with support, accountability, and resources as we grow and minister. God uses others to compliment us in areas where we are limited. We need one another.

In my life, I (Paul) have an upward mentoring relationship with Bobby Clinton. Each year I submit to him my written goals for the coming year. Each month or two I submit to him a written evaluation of goals. We also meet, write, or talk on the phone as time and circumstances permit. He has given me some very helpful counsel and has encouraged me in specific areas.

I also have lateral or peer mentoring relationships with several Christian pastors and leaders in the area where I live and in other locations. I have also submitted my written goals to them and periodically give them written or verbal updates. They also serve as support, encouragement, and resources for me. They keep me abreast of happenings in their organizations, challenging books they have read, people they have met, programs they have implemented, etc.

I also have formal and informal downward mentoring relationships with some of my students and a few younger emerging leaders. I learned a lot from Vernon about this range of mentoring so I always have my eyes open for young leaders who need some encouragement that they are getting started. Vernon's investment in me is now paying off in my investment in others.

Steps to Effective Upward Mentoring

For young Christians having a mentor can be tremendously helpful. But how do you go about finding the type of mentor you need? Good mentors are hard to find and bad mentoring can lead to all kinds of problems.

The first step in finding an upward mentor is to pray. Ask God what you need in a relationship and ask Him to provide the type of mentor you need. God may reveal to you that you need a type of mentoring very different from what you might have originally desired.

Often times, growth occurs best in difficult circumstances. Although we all need encouragement, we may also need someone who can speak to our weaknesses. Ron Lee Davis calls this tender-tough mentoring. This type of mentoring involves several aspects which he calls the seven cardinal rules of tender-tough mentoring. These rules include,

1. When you confront, be honest and direct.
2. When you confront, demonstrate unconditional love and acceptance.
3. When you confront, be specific. Never generalize.
4. When you confront, demonstrate empathy.
5. Build on the leader's strengths, gifts, and character through positive encouragement.
6. Affirm in public, correct in private.
7. Build an allegiance to relationships, not to issues. [24]

Within the context of this type of mentoring relationship a younger Christian and/or leader can get honest feedback, have the freedom to experiment without the risk of loosing the relationship, and grow from their experiences.

The second step is to **get involved**. Through prayer seek God for opportunities to get involved in people's lives and/or ministry. Be willing to serve in low profile situations such as

Sunday school classes, junior high ministry, or cleaning up the church after services.

It is within the context of involvement that God can bring people together in mentoring relationships. One of the things that I (Paul) look for in the young people that I mentor is a servant's heart attitude. Many want to be mentored but wait around hoping that it will come to them when they should be out there getting involved where the potential mentors are.

The third step is to be aware of the **attraction aspect of mentoring**. Attraction is the first dynamic of mentoring and becomes the initial step in developing a mentoring relationship. Mentors are attracted to "potential" leaders and "emerging" leaders are attracted to mentors. Attraction may lead to conversation, to working together, and possibly to some type of mentoring. Mentoring usually occurs within the natural circumstances of involvement and relationships.

The fourth step is to **clarify expectations** concerning mentoring. Be careful not to assume that because a potential mentor pays some attention to you in one setting that he/she is entering into a committed relationship of mentoring with you. The specifics of relationship and expectations need to be talked out and mutually agreed upon.

If expectations are not realistic and/or clearly formulated, there is all sorts of room for misunderstanding, hurt, and disillusionment. Some of this may occur even if expectations are clearly agreed upon because we are human and we fail from time to time.

When there are misunderstandings and hurt, we need to forgive and humbly and prayerfully work through the issues with the mentor. The working through of difficult issues can strengthen the relationship and build proper relational attitudes and skills into our lives.

The fifth and final step in securing upward mentoring is to be willing to take **personal responsibility** in the relationship. We must be careful not to develop an unhealthy dependence upon the mentor. We need to be open to the mentor and his/her input into our lives but we also need to learn to hear from and obey God.

Steps to Effective Peer Mentoring

Lateral or peer mentoring can be a real joy as we relate in meaningful ways with those who are part of our part of our generation, who face many of the same issues that we do, and who are moving ahead in response to God's call on their lives. Resources, cooperative involvement, shared experiences are all part of the benefits of lateral or peer mentoring and we all need them.

The steps for establishing peer mentoring are essentially the same as for upward mentoring. Prayer, involvement, attraction, clarification of expectations, and personal responsibility are important for effective peer mentoring. The major difference is in the area of authority and accountability.

In peer mentoring we relate to one another on a collegial or "equal" basis. We influence one another by who we are and there tends not to be an established hierarchy of authority. At times peer mentoring may involve accountability for certain aspects of behavior when mutually agreed upon.

Peer mentoring can be an exciting and effective way to care and be cared for. It is very easy for many of us to become isolated because of the demands on our lives. We will probably have to make peer mentoring a priority or it can be easily swallowed up by demands of our schedule. Peer mentoring can help us to stay relationally involved and learning as we face the challenges of our lives and ministries.

Steps to Effective Downward Mentoring

We may feel as though we are too young and/or inexperienced to mentor someone else. That was part of what young Timothy struggled with as he was pastoring the church at Ephesus. But Paul in his instructions to him reminded him not to "let anyone look down on you because you are young, but set an example for the believers in speech, in life, in love, in faith, and in purity" (I Timothy 4:12).

Remember that mentoring is one life touching another. As Christians we can be an example to others. We do not have to be perfect, just faithful. As Ted Engstrom has said, mentoring is an art. Mentoring, like all relationships, takes a lot of effort and must be cultivated over time. Regardless of age, we can touch other people's lives through our faithfulness.

Engstrom suggests four steps for effective "downward" mentoring. They are,

1. Select a mentoree whose philosophy of life you share. Our greatest mentors are those who are also our models.
2. Choose a person with potential you genuinely believe in... The secret of mentoring in any field is to help a person get to where he or she is willing to go.
3. Evaluate a mentoree's progress constantly. An honest mentor will be objective. If necessary he or she will encourage the person to stay on course, to seek another direction, or even to enter into a relationship with another mentor.
4. Be committed, serious, and available to mentorees.[25]

Final Exhortation

We have just scratched the surface of the issue of mentoring. There are numerous books that have been written which you will find very helpful. We encourage you to study them and begin a lifetime of mentoring relationships. Mentoring is one of the vital links in the chain of God's purpose for our lives and for the lives of those He is calling to lead in the next generation. *God uses people to empower other people for His highest purpose.* Paul encourages us to "carry each other's burdens, and in this way you will fulfill the law of Christ" (Galatians 6:2). It is not easy to make it through a lifetime of ministry. Without mentors, it is nearly impossible. For our own sake and the sake of younger emerging leaders, we need to find ways to be meaningfully involved in one another's lives. Meaningful mentor relationships can impact our lives and others in life changing ways.

Mentoring relationships are the primary place that we can be held accountable for our life, our growth and our ministries.

Accountability is sorely missing in most Christian leaders' lives. I believe that this has led to the downfall of many. We need to be held accountable. Who is holding you accountable?

Evaluation and Application

1. Prayerfully ask God whether or not you have the type(s) of mentoring you need in your life.

2. Reread the section(s) that pertain to your situation and look up all of the supporting passages while asking God to reveal Himself and His purposes to you. Write down your insights and ask God how He wants you to apply these insights. Write down a strategy for applying these insights, act on them, and evaluate.

3. Begin to systematically study the lives of Biblical, historical, and contemporary Christian leaders in order to learn from them.

4. Pick up the book *Connecting* by Bobby Clinton and Paul Stanley. Study the issues and dynamics of effective mentoring. Begin to use them in your life.

---

[1] Paul Stanley and J. Robert Clinton, Connecting, Colorado Springs, CO: Navpress, 1992, p. 33.

[2] J. Robert Clinton, The Mentor Handbook, Altadena, CA: Barnabas Publishers, 1992, p. 24.

[3] A. B. Bruce, The Training of the Twelve, Grand Rapids, MI: Kregel Publications, 1971, 1988, p. 11-12.

[4] Ron Lee Davis, Mentoring: The Strategy of the Master, Nashville, TN: Thomas Nelson Publishers, 1991, p. 33.

[5] Clinton, (1992), p. 26.

[6] Clinton and Stanley, p. 42.

[7] Clinton and Stanley, p. 48.

[8] John Robertson, Timothy Principle, Colorada Springs, CO: Navpress, 1986, p. 83.

[9] Youth With A Mission, Discipleship Training School (DTS)

[10] Clinton and Stanley, p. 65.

[11] Foster, Celebration of Discipline. p. 9.

[12] Clinton and Stanley, p. 79.

[13] Alan Loy McGinnis, <u>Bringing Out the Best in People</u>, Augsburg Publishing, 1985, p. 10.

[14] Clinton and Stanley, p. 95-96.

[15] Larry Crabb, <u>Effective Biblical Counseling</u>. Grand Rapids, MI: Zondervan, 1977, p. 22.

[16] Clinton and Stanley, p. 95-96.

[17] Howard Hendricks, <u>Teaching to Change Lives</u>. Portland, OR: Multnomah Press and Walk Thru the Bible Ministries, 1987, p. 119.

[18] Hendricks, p. 121-122.

[19] Clinton and Stanley, p. 124-125.

[20] Ted Engstrom, <u>The Fine Art of Mentoring</u>. Brentwood, TN: Wolgemuth and Hyatt Publishers, 1978, p. 2.

[21] Clinton and Stanley, p. 143.

[22] Clinton and Stanley, p. 147.

[23] Clinton and Stanley, see chapter 11, p. 157-168.

[24] Davis, see chapter 4.

[25] Engstrom, p. 24.

10

The Issue of Destiny

I (Richard) will never forget an experience that I had one afternoon in the summer of 1985. I was nearly two years into a church plant when a leader from another church asked if we could get together to pray. She said that she felt that God had something that He wanted to say to me. I had watched this leader minister in a number of situations and knew that she was sensitive to the Holy Spirit and that God used her in prophetic ministry. Nothing that I had experienced previously had prepared me for what happened that afternoon. This prayer time together was unlike any other prayer time that I had ever experienced.

We sat down together in her living room and began to pray. She began to pray about things that she felt God was going to do in my life. For the first 20 minutes or so, she prayed about nothing but character issues. She asked God to work deeply in my life and that things like integrity, honesty, obedience, genuineness and faithfulness would become major characteristics of my life. At the end of this time, she felt that God wanted to speak directly to me. She became quiet.

As soon as she was quiet, I began to sense the powerful presence of the Holy Spirit. In an inner voice, I began to hear God speak to me about the future. God began to speak to me about what He was going to take me through in the future and why it was important that I learn to respond faithfully to Him.

Along with these words, I saw several visions in my mind's eye. God explained what each vision meant. I don't really know how long this lasted but near the end of this exchange between God and I, the leader who was praying with me began to pray.

She began by saying, "This is what you have just seen and heard." Then without me saying a word, she described the visions that I had seen and described the essence of what God had just spoken to me. Needless to say, I was stunned. I really didn't know what to make of the experience. I had never had an experience quite like this one before.

I walked away from that experience pondering the things that I believed God had shown me. To be honest, I was a little confused and frightened by what I believed God had said about me and the future. It wasn't until about two months later that I wrote down my thoughts and feelings about this experience.

What I have just described is what I call a sense of destiny experience. It has been nearly 10 years since that experience. Over that time, many things have happened to confirm what God revealed to me on that summer afternoon. God has continued to clarify and reveal things about what He is doing and what He plans to do in and through me. I realize that my part of God's plan is to keep responding positively to Him and to learn the lessons that He wants me to learn. God has used this experience in a number of powerful ways over the last 10 years.

What is a sense of destiny? Does everyone have one? How do you know when God is revealing some aspect of your destiny? In this chapter, I am going to address these questions and more. The issue of destiny is a crucial one for developing leaders. *I believe that God will cultivate a sense of destiny in each leader*. Over time, He will reveal His special plans for that leader as He moves to develop him/her. God can use this sense of destiny to encourage leaders and motivate them to respond in faith.

What is a sense of destiny?

A sense of destiny is an inner conviction. The conviction is that God is involved in a special way developing and preparing the leader so that he/she can accomplish His special purposes during his/her lifetime. This inner conviction comes as a result of experiences in which the leader becomes aware that God has intervened in a personal and special way in order to encourage the development of the leader. Often the leader is not aware of this "destiny" during the beginning stages of his/her leadership. The leader's destiny is revealed over time. As God reveals his/ her destiny through a variety of means, the leader becomes increasingly aware of it.

As we have studied various leaders' lives here at Fuller Seminary, we have been able to discern a pattern of development related to a sense of destiny. There are three parts of the pattern. We call them destiny preparation, destiny revelation, and destiny fulfillment.

Destiny Preparation

Destiny preparation involves those experiences where God does a preparatory work in the leader's life which gives the leader a growing sense that God wants to use him/her in some special way. These experiences are understood when looked at in retrospect. These type of destiny experiences serve to instill in the leader that there is a special purpose that God has for him/ her. That is, they prepare a leader for his/her destiny.

There are a number of Biblical incidents which provide illustrations of preparatory items. For example, Hannah's contract with God regarding a son was certainly a destiny preparation item for Samuel. How many times do you think Samuel heard that story when he was growing up? Just the fact that he grew up away from his parents would have been significant enough to warrant the telling of the story. Moses' parents defied the order of the Pharaoh and saved his life. The fact that he survived when every other Hebrew son his own age was killed gave Moses a sense of significance to his life. How many times do you think that he asked himself the question, "why did I survive"?

Destiny preparation items are any significant acts, people, providential circumstances or a special sense of timing that hint at some future significance to a life. Here are some of the kinds of destiny preparation items that we have run across in our research of leaders:

- prophecies spoken over children that the parents record and tell the child as they grow up

- *a special name given to a child*

- a parent's conviction about God using the child in a special way. This conviction is articulated to the child in some way.

- a contract or oath between the parent and God concerning the child

- unusual birth circumstances (in some way, it is evident that God has intervened and spared the child's life or given a child when it didn't seem possible)

- the preservation of life (near death through sickness or accidents often add a sense of significance to a person's life)

- a Godly heritage. There seems to be something that is passed on from one generation to the next that adds a sense of significance and a feeling of special usefulness to God.

All of these types of experience in retrospect can give a person a sense of preparation for being used by God in a special way.

Destiny Revelation

The second aspect of the destiny pattern is called destiny revelation. These types of experiences move a leader from a general awareness that God wants to use them in a special way to specific convictions about it. Destiny revelation describes any experience during which God confirms that the leader has a special destiny and begins to reveal or clarify what that special purpose might be.

There are numerous illustrations of destiny revelation in the Scriptures. Joseph's dreams give him a sense of the future and his role as it related to his family. These dreams also got him into a lot of trouble with his brothers. Abraham's encounters with God during which God revealed the great promise of a son and a people. Moses' experience at the burning bush was a powerful instance of confirmation and clarification that God wanted to use him in a special way. David's encounter with Samuel when he was anointed with oil by the prophet is another example. Paul's encounter with Jesus and then Ananias in Damascus were destiny revelation experiences for Paul. God confirmed His special plan for Paul by confirming it through Ananias.

In our research at Fuller with leaders, we have run across the following types of destiny revelation experiences. Each of the following types of experiences can be used by God to reveal a leader's destiny.

- God gives the leader a dream or vision concerning the future.

- God gives the leader a prophetic word about the future.

- the leader during a time of reflection or evaluation makes an intuitive insight about his/her destiny.

- God uses an experience in which the leader is challenged in some way to respond in faith or with Godly character to reveal some aspect of a future destiny. The leader sees a direct connection between the situation and some future ministry.

- some powerful guidance experiences with God. Moments of decision making are key times for God to speak and lead clearly toward some future destiny.

- in a power encounter situation or some situation where God's power is released in ministry, the leader is used by God in such a way that the leader catches a glimpse of future involvement in ministry. God often uses these types of experiences as catalytic moments in a leader's life.

- when God answers a prayer request in a specific way, the leader often feels a sense of affirmation that can lead to the realization that he/she is moving in the right direction.

Destiny Fulfillment

Destiny fulfillment describes significant acts, people, and circumstances which represent the completion of some aspect of a person's destiny that was revealed previously. When Joseph's brothers came and bowed down before him in Egypt, he knew that the dreams (destiny revelation) had been fulfilled. Joseph recognized that the final act of destiny would be for his bones to be buried in his homeland. This aspect of his destiny was fulfilled when Joshua led God's people into the land. When Paul wrote a letter to Timothy near the end of his life, he was able to reflect back on his life and ministry and see that he had lived out the destiny that God had set before him. He finished his race and was obedient to what God had called him to do.

Destiny fulfillment is usually seen later in life and ministry as a person looks back and reflects on what God has done during the leader's lifetime. The person can view both the initial promise of God and the fulfillment of that promise over the course of his/her lifetime. It is possible to see progress along the way. There can be little indications along the way that demonstrate that a leader is following the destiny that God has set out.

I remember nearly 11 years ago about a time when God revealed a part of my future destiny during a prayer time. I saw a vision in my mind's eyes of myself leading meetings in other countries. I saw two locations in particular. The vision was vivid. I saw this vision before God called me into the pastorate. I was simply attending a small group and during a prayer time, God "surprised" me by showing me a picture of some future ministry that I was going to be involved in. At the time, I was greatly encouraged and took it as a confirming encouraging word to keep pursuing God and His ministry. About three years later, I did lead a team overseas and led a ministry meeting in one of the locations that I had seen in that vision. Two years later on another trip, I got the privilege of leading some ministry in the other location. These two incidents in a small way represented destiny fulfillment for me. God used this experience to greatly encourage me. These little indications of destiny fulfillment serve as deposits of hope and increase my faith to continue responding to God as

I move toward other aspects of His destiny for me.

Answering Some Important Questions

There are a number of questions that commonly are asked about "a sense of destiny". Destiny is a word full of hope to many. Others are frightened by the future and don't want to think about it. It certainly prompts many questions. Here are some of the most common questions:

1. Is this idea of "a sense of destiny" Biblical?

In my opinion, God makes it very clear that each one of us have a special purpose in His kingdom. In Ephesians 2:10, Paul writes about the fact that God has "hand-crafted" each one of us *so that* we might accomplish God's purposes. God has established His purposes before time as we know it. Overall, God is working out in His redemptive drama. He is reconciling the world to Him through the work of Jesus. He has chosen to use nations, certain structures, peoples, and individuals to be involved in this reconciling work. As individuals, we can choose to respond to this Divine design and enter into a life of obedience. He has special purposes for each one of us. Each person's unique destiny (God's purposes) vary depending on circumstances, our place in life, the times in which we live, our unique giftedness and God's sovereign plan.

Think about the lives of important leaders in the Biblical accounts. How did God reveal their special destiny to them before they moved into it? As you seek the answer to this question, you will discover the idea that God initiated activity which helped impart "a sense of destiny" to people throughout the Scriptures. You will see how God led the various leaders in the Bible through a variety of experiences which imparted a sense of destiny to them..

2. Why should I worry about the future by trying to think about my destiny?

I have found that many leaders struggle with the idea of seeking what God wants to do with them in the future. They have adopted a posture which says "I'm don't want to know about the future, I have enough to worry about with today's problems. Thinking about a sense of destiny just adds extra pressure that I don't think I can handle." I would respond to this kind of posture by saying that having God hint at or reveal some aspect of your future destiny can be an affirming, stimulating and encouraging experience. God does not hint at or reveal pieces of our destiny to confuse us but rather to encourage us and to help us build faith. God often uses destiny revelation experiences to test our "faith responses".

If thinking about the future causes you to become anxious or causes you to worry; in my opinion, it is an issue of trust and faith. Because God loves us, He reveals what He is doing or going to do. We can trust Him. We can find our strength in His sovereign purposes. In my understanding, God initiates and we respond. We don't have to "make our own destiny". It is not our initiative. Because God loves us, He shows us what He is doing with us. We respond in faith to His initiative as He works out our destiny. This understanding helps me to alleviate any anxiety or worry that might come as I contemplate the future. We all need to have a "vision for the future". Without it, we will lose hope and will become discouraged. I believe that God leads us through these destiny experiences in order to impart hope and vision for the future.

3. Does everyone have a "sense of destiny"?

The answer is yes and no. At this point, I think it is helpful to distinguish between leaders and followers. Every leader that we have studied has reported how God revealed His destiny for them through a wide variety of experiences. Each leader had some kind of a "sense of destiny". Some leaders had a highly developed sense of destiny. What I mean is that these leaders were very aware of God's destiny for them. Others did not. For those who had a highly developed sense of destiny, God used it to motivated them to pursue God's work in faith.

On the other hand, many of the leaders that we have studied initially do not think they have any "sense of destiny". These leaders when first exposed to the notion of a sense of destiny respond by saying, "I don't have one!" However, as they begin to reflect back on their life and ministry, they find that God has given them hints and indications of His destiny for them along the way. They simply have never thought about it or paid attention to the various experiences. In hindsight, with a little help, they can begin to see how God has been involved in their lives and how He has been revealing their destiny. Because of this, we are leaning strongly to the side of saying that every leader at some level has a sense of destiny. Some leaders have a highly developed awareness of it. Others do not. Also, it is important to remember that God imparts a sense of destiny over time and the leader's faithful responses do make a difference in his/her development.

Does every person have a "sense of destiny"? I'm not sure. At this point, I believe that everyone has to have at least some general feelings about his/her destiny. Being a part of God's kingdom and His redemptive drama would generate this level or feeling of destiny in each one of us. We are part of God's redemptive work in the world. God wants to use each one of us in His kingdom work. Beyond this, I'm not sure how specific the "average" person in a church will be aware of his/her sense of destiny.

4. How does the sense of destiny differ from a call to ministry?

Often, when people hear about the "sense of destiny idea", they think that we are talking about a person's call to ministry. A person's call to ministry experience is certainly an important destiny experience but destiny includes more than just this experience. A call to ministry can be a general thing. For example, a person might be called to be a pastor. God will need to reveal some other important information along the way. Where are you to pastor? In what denomination or with what group and why? What type of leadership are you to offer? How does God want to use your unique giftedness, personality and experiences? What unique contributions does God want to give the body of Christ through your service?

5. Isn't promoting this idea of destiny dangerous, especially with younger leaders?

Yes, it can be dangerous because it can lead to an inflated view of yourself. It can lead to some spiritual pride in younger leaders. It can lead to a focus on self. However, I have found that God usually corrects these kinds of problems by taking the leader through several experiences which will "break" this kind of attitude or spiritual pride.

I have found that people who try to promote themselves in the kingdom of God don't get very far. Even if the person has tremendous natural abilities and a powerful personality, they will be "exposed" eventually. They may seem to be effective and powerful in the ministry for a while but eventually what they really are will show up. People will recognize that these kinds of leaders are operating in their own strength and God is not with them.

Think about this from a different perspective. The emerging generation of leaders who are in their teens and twenties right now need to know that God can use them. This generation has been beaten down by life. For the most part, they have lost hope in having a meaningful role in the future. While it may be dangerous to promote this idea to younger leaders who have tendencies to think more of themselves than they should, there are an increasing number of younger leaders who need to know that their lives can count. Their lives are important and God has something special for them. They need the encouragement that a sense of destiny imparts because it brings a sense of hope and expectation to them.

6. How do you recognize destiny experiences and what do you do with them?

Begin by asking God to help you. Simply, being aware that God does reveal a person's destiny over time through any number of experiences is the starting place. Learning to sensitize yourself to recognize important incidents, experiences with God and God's people is important.

You will want to spend some time reflecting back over your life and ministry to this point. What situations, important incidents or people has God used to confirm the fact that He wants to use you to accomplish His purposes? A helpful place to start is your call to ministry. How did God call you to the ministry? How do you know? Was it specific or general? Had God led you through any experiences which have confirmed this call to ministry? Have you had anyone speak any types of prophetic words over you about your future? Have you had any special times alone with God in which you felt that He showed you something about your future? Have you had any dreams or visions that you believed God gave you concerning the future? Have you had any experiences in ministry where you felt a sense of God's affirmation and felt encouraged to continue? Questions like these and others like them will sensitize you to identifying sense of destiny experiences. If you go through these questions and still find yourself frustrated or anxious about this destiny idea, don't worry about it. Ask God to lead you and direct you. He will.

It is well worth the time and effort to record incidents from your past which either were preparing you to recognize that God had a destiny for you or revealed what that destiny was in some way. Then, be sensitive to experiences that may be sense of destiny experiences. There have been many times that I went through some kind of experience that I wasn't sure about. I record as many as possible. You never know when you are in a situation whether or not God is saying something. I have found that it is safer to write down a description of what happened or what was said and put it in the file. I can always come back later and take it out and reflect on the incident. I go through my own file once a year and keep what I know came from God and take out some of the stuff that obviously wasn't from God.

I want to add just a note about personal prophecies. Personal prophecies are prophetic words that are given to an individual which concern the future of that individual. Over recent years, there has been an increasing number of ministries which involve giving personal prophecies. I myself have been involved over the last few years in both receiving and giving these types of prophetic words to people. I have found these types of situations to be very encouraging if they are taken in the proper context. In my opinion, God releases these types of words to encourage us.

At the same time, I have learned over the years that these type of situations can cause a lot of confusion. In my experience (on both sides), I have found that the prophetic words have complex variables which can generate a little confusion for the people involved. These words are made up of a mixture of revelatory information from God. What I mean is that a part of the word comes from God and it is mixed with other things. The initial word from the Lord is genuine and accurate. But there are other factors that influence the giving of that word.

The word is often interpreted by the prophetic person. It is interpreted by the individual receiving the word. Or other people involved with the individual help interpret the word. There may be slight differences between the various interpretations. If the prophetic word involves some type of response, the people involved need to make an application of the word. On top of this, there are the feelings and thoughts of the people involved. In other words, there are a lot of variables which can be easily misinterpreted.

It takes time to learn to discern accurately what God is saying. It is not wise to take each of these "words" and assume them to be "words from God". Personally, I have learned to take these types of words both seriously and not seriously at the same time. Here is how I do that. I always begin by assuming that God has given the prophetic words as encouragement from God. I carefully record what happened in each situation along with any thoughts or feelings that I may have had. Then, I just watch and wait. If the "essence" of the prophetic word was from God, He will initiate situations where I can respond in faith. I will be able to recognize and move. In other words, you can't make it happen. The primary response of faith involves recognizing what God is doing and moving in cooperation with it.

7. What if I have a huge sense of destiny? What do I do between now and then?

From time to time, I run across individuals who have a huge sense of destiny. I have observed two basic types of people. Some individuals feel overwhelmed by what he/she believes God has told them about the future. Their "sense of destiny" is overwhelming to them. Others have a huge sense of destiny and it causes them to be a little full of pride or naive about the process of leadership development.

To both kinds of individuals, I counsel the same thing...engage the process. I ask them these kinds of questions: if what you believe God is showing you is true, what character qualities will it take to accomplish that destiny? If what you believe God is showing you is true, what kinds of lessons or wisdom will need to be learned? If what you believe God is showing you is true, what kinds of ministry experiences will help you prepare for it? The bottom line is: how would God prepare a leader for ...(whatever it is that they have described). This is what I mean by engaging the process. The answers to those types of questions will take up the time between now and then.

As a leader, you can not make your destiny happen. God is the initiator and we are the responders. We can block or hinder God's destiny for us by poor choices or responses. Faithful and Godly responses to God's initiative will move you toward the destiny that God has for you.

8. What difference does it make knowing about this destiny thing?

There are three major reasons why I believe that leaders should be sensitized to discovering their sense of destiny. The first reason is that having a sense of destiny will be a source of encouragement during tough times. Every leader who has been involved in ministry for more than a day or two knows that leadership and ministry can be very challenging and difficult. From time to time we need to be able to step back from the day to day grind and see how what we are doing today is involved in where God is leading us. Being aware of destiny revelation will provide the perspective that we need.

I can personally testify to the great encouragement that I have received from my own sense of destiny experiences during challenging and tough times. I have made it a practice to keep track of experiences which I think might be sense of destiny experiences. I write up a brief description of each incident and have put them all in a file. From time to time, I pull out this file and review all of the descriptions of the destiny experiences. During times of transition and difficult moments, this file has provided great encouragement.

The second reason deals with guidance and decision making. My sense of destiny file has helped me to focus in on some key issues when I am trying to make a decision about life or ministry. When I am in a situation where I need to make a decision, I read through the file and check to see whether or not it can help me.

There have been two very difficult transitions recently in which my sense of destiny file provided focus and insight into what I was going through and why I was going through it. God had led me through several destiny experiences which prepared me for the transition. I had written down a description of the incident although at the time I didn't understand what God was saying or doing. However, a few months later as I was in the midst of the crisis, the incidents made complete sense and the Lord's direction became clear. As we get a little farther along in our leadership development, we can use our sense of destiny experiences to help us make decisions which allow us to move in cooperation with what God is doing.

The third reason deals with our response to God's destiny for us. As I have mentioned, God initiates and we respond. One of the ways that we can respond to what God reveals to us is to become proactive in our training. We can seek training and develop skills in areas that we believe that God is leading us toward. We can get involved in ministry experiences which will develop us in the right direction. We can prepare ourselves for what we believe God is leading us toward. This creates a sense of cooperation between God and the leader. It is a response of faith.

Summary

God has a special destiny for each one of us. As emerging leaders, we need to be aware that God will hint at and reveal what He is doing with us. He will lead us through a number of experiences which He will use to communicate to us. We need to be sensitive to recognizing these experiences. Cultivating a sense of destiny will allow you to move in cooperation with where God is leading you. It allows you to proactively embrace training and learn lessons that will help you as you move toward accomplishing the destiny that God has for you.

I'd like to end this chapter with a couple of little stories. These stories are about two people that God loves. Recently I was on a trip where I was ministering to a group of young emerging leaders. In that context, I was able to counsel and pray with a number of individuals. Two of them stick out in my mind. I am excited about what God is doing in each one of them.

The first person was a young woman who was struggling with her relationship with God. She felt that God could not use her or that there was no real hope for her future because of her past. God gave me insight into her situation through a prophetic word in which God called her out. He gave me a word (a personal prophecy) about how God viewed her and His purposes for her future. God cut right to the heart of the issue. She had lost hope and didn't feel that God could be close to her. Our time together was a destiny experience for her. She walked away from the situation greatly encouraged. From her point of view, God had identified her to a complete stranger (me), had told him about her situation and had given him insight and an encouraging word. She walked away with a fresh dose of hope and expectation about God's involvement in her future...her destiny.

In the same meeting, a young man walked up and introduced himself to me. I could tell by the way he spoke and the way that he carried himself that confidence was not a problem for him. He had a few questions about leadership and leadership development. He began by telling me that God had revealed to him that he was going to be a "worldwide evangelist". God had spoken to him and called him to win the world! I could tell by the way that he shared "his call" that other leaders had listened to his story and dismissed it and him. I listened to his questions and asked him quietly how he liked the desert...the wilderness. He didn't understand the question. I elaborated. I said that if God was going to use him in the way that he believed God had revealed to him, then there was going to be quite a process of training and preparation. I shared with him that God loved to use the desert (wilderness) and isolation (hiddenness) as training ground. The desert purifies, illuminates and cleanses. I asked him if he was willing to go into the desert with God. As you can imagine, my questions caught him a little off guard. He had a huge sense of destiny. I do believe that God had placed a tremendous call on his life. What he didn't have was the perspective of what it took to get from here to there. His encounter was another type of destiny experience. In essence, I validated what he was sharing with me about his future by challenging him to go deep with God. I counseled him to focus on the process of development, not the end result.

What has God said to you about your future destiny in His kingdom? Why are you here? What is God doing with you? The issue of destiny is important. During the first ten years of ministry, every leader will be challenged in this area. God will test the resolve of each leader. It takes perseverance to make it to the end, to finish well. Remember that one of the characteristics of a leader who had finished well is that he/she has fulfilled in some aspect the destiny that God laid out for his/her life. It is wise to take the time and effort to evaluate what God has said and what God is revealing to you about your future.

Evaluation and Application:

1. Take the following three leaders (Joseph, David, Paul) and analyze their lives in terms of destiny. In what ways did God prepare them for His plan? How did God reveal His plans to them? What insights can you learn about destiny

by studying God's activity in their lives?

2. Have a discussion about the "dangers of destiny". Talk about the issues of spiritual pride, false hopes and expectations, and the sense of drivenness that is unhealthy. Explore how each of these issues impact your own life and understanding. What can you do to guard against them?

3. Have a discussion about the positive benefits of being aware of your destiny. Talk about the issues of motivation, faith, hope, purpose and meaning, and learning to respond in faith. Explore how each of these issues impacts your own life and understanding. How can you allow your awareness of destiny to encourage you and build you up?

4. Spend time reflecting back over your life. In what ways has God prepared you or revealed His plans (your destiny) to you? Write down as many incidents and situations as you can. Describe them and evaluate what God might have been saying to you. Begin to keep a journal or file of these situations.

11

Strategies for Starting Well

The writing of this book has been a wonderful project for me. I (Richard) have been forced to do a lot of reflection and evaluation concerning my first ten years in ministry. I have marveled as I worked through each chapter at all of the things God has done to bring me to this point. *He is a faithful and loving God!* He will be faithful to you as well!

In this final chapter, I want to suggest a basic strategy that might help you in your efforts to start well as an emerging leader. A strategy is a plan or a method for obtaining a specific result or objective. We started this book by outlining what "finishing well" was. Finishing well as we have defined it is a worthy objective. It is the result of a life that is lived for God and a life that is lived well.

Bobby Clinton speaks about finishing well and calls it "living a focused life". He defines a focused life as "a life that is dedicated to exclusively carrying out God's unique purposes through it."[1] God's unique purposes are identified by various means which Bobby Clinton calls focal issues. As the leader increasingly recognizes and identifies the focus of his/her life and ministry, he/she moves toward that focus in a deliberate way. He/she makes choices which show an increasing prioritization of his/her activities around God's focus. Living a focused life will bring complete satisfaction in every way.

The "focus" may look a little different for each one of us. There are some things that are the same for all of us. For example, we know from Scripture that God is shaping our "beingness" (what we are) to be like Christ. Each of us is to be Christlike in our character. We know that God is going to initiate the process of transformation in each one of us.

"Doingness" (what we do) is a little more complicated because of the uniqueness factor. God creates and develops each one of us to be unique individuals. He gives us unique personalities, unique gifts and abilities, unique life experiences, unique opportunities and a unique context out of which to operate. Discovering exactly what God wants us to "do" involves a process of discovery that takes into account all of the various factors that I have listed above. The key is recognizing that God wants us to discover how our uniqueness operates and He is committed to revealing His special destiny for each one of us. God takes the initiative in this process of discovery. We can live a focused life. God will lead us into it and establish us in it. Our job is responding to Him in ways that honor Him.

Having said this, you can see that I can't outline a strategy that is unique to you. Instead, I will touch on some basic aspects of a plan or strategy that will help you grow and mature into the person or the leader that God wants. My suggestions cover the most important things that I have learned during the first ten years of ministry. I am not going to try to list them in any order of importance. Rather, I am just going to touch on them one at a time.

However, I first want to highlight three important lessons. These lessons encompass the major points of this book.

Three Philosophical Foundations

First, whether you consider yourself to be an emerging leader or not, God has a special purpose for you. Because He loves you, He has made a way for you to be with Him. He wants relationship with you. You get to participate in His redemptive drama. He has a role for you in His kingdom. He has equipped you with a unique personality, a unique giftedness and has placed you in your context for a reason. Over the course of your lifetime, you want to discover and move toward God's focus for your life. As you move in cooperation with Him and His purposes for you, you will be fully satisfied and content with life.

Second, our development as people and as leaders occurs over a lifetime. God initiates shaping activity by using circumstances, people and situations to develop us in different ways. He wants to shape our character to be like Christ. He wants to shape us so that we can learn the skills that we need to serve and minister in His kingdom. He wants to shape us so that we can understand Him and His principles and live according to them.

Third, we get to respond to His shaping activity. Our response determines how we are developed and matured. We need to take an active learning posture. We need to learn about God and His ways. We need to learn about ourselves and our uniqueness. We need to learn about relating to others in God honoring ways. If we maintain a healthy learning posture, God will teach us and develop us. Life will be our teacher. Experience will be our teacher. Others will teach us. We will discover truth.

These three lessons serve as the philosophical foundation for all that we have written here. Any strategy that we might present has these three basic philosophical lessons as their foundation.

Key Aspects of A Strategy for Development

Developing A Biblical Image of God

A.W.Tozer says, "What comes into our minds when we think about God is the most important thing about us."[2] This is an arresting quote. I have found that what I think about God, my image of God, influences everything that I think and do. This is especially true as I think about my personal relationship with Him and my ministry to others. Let me illustrate what I mean by this.

What you think about God is reflected in the way you deliver your ministry. Several years ago, I went through what I call a "brokenness" experience. Others call it a refining fire or a stripping away. Without going into the circumstances that led me to this place, let me say that circumstances had pushed me into it. I was in a crisis like I had never faced before. I found myself alone with God in a way that I had never experienced before. I had nothing to fall back on. I, for the first time in my life, recognized how truly bankrupt I was before God. There were no resources that I could draw on to give me strength. I was truly at the end of my own energy and resources. I had done everything to fix my circumstances. There was nothing further that I could do and I was ready to give up. I remember one night being in a place of deep despair.

In this place of inner silence and terrible aloneness, God met me. He knew pain. He offered me companionship. He didn't offer me any words of explanation. He offered to walk with me. It has taken years of walking together for me to begin the process of recovery.

Probably the most significant thing that happened in this experience is that my image of God was exposed for what it was. From that time until now, I have been in a process of discovering who God is and what He is like. Before this experience, my basic image of God was that He was someone who demanded everything to be perfect and fixed before you could approach Him. I viewed Him as distant and hard to get to. He was a God who only listened to prayers that were offered by "pure" people. My job was to be pure and righteous so that I could get close to Him. I could quote all the attributes of God from the systematic theology courses but there was a difference between my theology and my real viewpoint. Can any of you relate to this?

Before I experienced pain and bankruptcy before God, I treated the people that I was ministering to in the same way that I expected God to treat me. I knew that He accepted me because of His grace and mercy but once that initial acceptance was realized, I needed to take the initiative to clean up my act. My image of God controlled my understanding of ministry and influenced my relationships with people.

In the brokenness experience, God began the process of revealing to me who He is and what He is like. I was overwhelmed by His love. I was overwhelmed by His pain. He was a God who suffered and hurt. He was a God who was near to those who hurt. He is one who embraces the hurting and wounded. He is the Healer.

As my image of God began to change, I found that I began to see others differently as well. No longer were issues as black and white. I found that I was much quicker to extend mercy and grace and love.

Over the past seven years, I have been intentionally studying the Scriptures to understand who God is and what God is like. I especially like the word pictures that the Scriptures use to help us understand God. I have spent time in the last month studying the gospel of John and meditating on the "I am" passages.

There are many ways to work on establishing a Biblical image of God. For example, you might want to start by reading the Psalms and meditating on the various images of God that are used. You could study the names of God that are used in the Bible. No matter what method you choose to start with, I would encourage you to intentionally work on this. Your image of God will influence the way you relate to God. It will influence the way you minister to others. It is the starting place of relationship.

Cultivating A Relationship With God

Developing a Biblical image of God is the starting place of building your relationship with God. Cultivating this relationship takes time and effort. It is worth the effort and discipline. It is in the context of relationship that we are transformed and empowered to live and minister to others. There is no shortcut and no substitution for the relationship building process.

Learning to practice the spiritual disciplines is very helpful in building a relationship with God. It takes discipline to build relationship. Developing intimacy in our relationship is the goal. As we draw near to God, He draws near to us. We commune with Him. He gives us strength and perspective about our life and what He is doing in us and through us.

There are many "how to" books that have been written about building a relationship with God.   There are many different approaches that are advocated by different groups. The key components of your relationship should revolve around His word, talking to Him, and spending time with Him.   People with different temperaments and personalities will be drawn to different approaches and practicing certain disciplines.

For leaders, there is nothing that can be substituted for learning the Word of God. As leaders, we need to be immersed in His word. The Bible clearly reveals God. We need to be able to understand what God says about Himself. Certain leaders (those who have responsibility for teaching and preaching) need to know the Scriptures thoroughly.

The basic point is that we all need to develop intimacy in our relationship with God. Our relationship with God affects all that we are and all that we do. Investing in this relationship is crucial during the first ten years of ministry and leadership development. Taking the time necessary will run counter to the natural tendencies that most leaders have during the early stages of ministry. Most leaders find themselves wrapped up in "busyness".   Taking time to nurture and build relationship is relegated to spare time, which there never seems to be enough of. We need to guard against this tendency.

Engaging the Process of Character Transformation

You will notice that this aspect of strategy involves relationship with God as well. Life and ministry flow out of relationship with Him. Integrity doesn't happen by chance. It must be worked on and learned. It has to be established by choices that we make. The same could be said about obedience, humility, faith and faithfulness.

God will initiate His shaping activity to help you learn to live and operate with Godly character. He is committed to the process. He will be watching your responses. He will promote the people who respond positively to Him.

Be proactive in your responses. Be sensitive to the Holy Spirit as He guides you through various situations. Determine ahead of time that you are going to respond in Godly ways.

The Importance of Mentors

We have written an entire chapter on the importance of mentoring so I won't elaborate on it at this point.   It is wise to surround yourself with mentors who can hold you accountable for your growth, your actions and your relationships.

A few years ago I heard an interesting report during one of my doctoral courses.   The professor (Dr. Archibald Hart) was talking about the personal development of pastors. He was addressing the issue of burnout in the ministry. He told us that research was being done in this area. He reported some of the preliminary findings.   He said that the figures were still being researched and documented but the initial reports were pretty staggering. He mentioned that only about one in four people who graduated from seminary and went into the pastorate didn't burnout in the first five years. In other words, three out of four pastors burned out in the first five years. Most of these pastors dropped out of the ministry.   He went on to say that of the pastors who didn't burn out in the first five years only half of them made it to the ten year mark without burning out.   He shared that the majority of people who graduated with master of divinity degrees were no longer in the ministry ten years after graduation. He went on to share reasons why he believed that pastors were burning out at such a dramatic rate. Just before the end of the lecture he slipped in a comment that made me sit straight up. He shared that *every single one of the pastors who did not burn out in the first ten years of ministry attributed this to the fact that they had a significant mentor who helped them through.*

We need the perspective and wisdom that upward mentors can share with us. We need their direction to help guide us through the delicate situations in ministry that could cause us to burnout. We need peer mentors who can encourage us and share our frustrations, victories and walk with us. Most importantly, peer mentors can help us battle the loneliness of ministry. We need downward mentors to challenge us with their idealism and enthusiasm. They will encourage us to articulate what we have learned in ways that will help us understand ourselves better.

I would say that establishing a balanced network of mentoring relationships is a priority during the first ten years of ministry. It will take time and energy but will without a doubt be worth it.

The Issue of Accountability

Accountability is a negative concept to many emerging leaders. I have heard a few say things like, "I am accountable to God. I don't have to answer to anyone." When I hear things like this, I recognize that this young leader doesn't understand what accountability is all about or how important it is.

Accountability involves relationship and having another person or people know you well enough to encourage you to grow. Accountability involves someone checking up on you to see if you are honoring the commitments that you have made. It could be commitments to God, to yourself, to your spouse, to your friends, to your ministry or to others.

Having someone hold you accountable implies that you have set some goals or made some commitments. I want to talk about goal setting and growth projects. Some people love to set goals. Others are scared to death to do it. I have actually experienced both of these. For about six years now, I have been setting yearly growth goals. At first I was fearful of the discipline involved and I wondered how I would respond if I didn't do well. My upward mentor really helped me in this regard. He had me set goals that were relationship oriented and task oriented. He encouraged me to use the goals as guidelines rather than taskmasters. Over the years, these goals have been extremely valuable to my personal growth. Let me tell you why.

I use the experience of goal setting as a way to measure my growth. I use my goals as guidelines. Here is how I write out yearly goals. I use the calendar year because it seems like a normal time for reflection and evaluation. I usually begin the process of praying about the coming year sometime around October or November.

In my times of prayer, I begin to ask God what He wants me to focus on in my spiritual growth as well as other areas such as my family relationships or responsibilities with my job. Over the past three years, God has given me a theme for spiritual growth and exploration. For example, last year (1993) God spoke to me about developing in prophetic intercession and ministry. This involved a number of activities that related to developing sensitivity to the Holy Spirit in prayer. I had to establish disciplines of solitude and silence in order to learn to hear what God was saying. I worked on developing a sense of intimacy in my prayer life. I also had to work on responding in obedience when I felt prompted to do something about what I believed God was showing me. This year (1994) God has been speaking about the issue of faith and building faith. I am in the midst of wrestling with what this means. I have discovered issues in my own life that hinder my ability to respond to God in faith. I am exploring with God's help how to overcome these issues.

I intentionally allow myself freedom to eliminate some of the goals that don't fit over the course of the year or to add others that become appropriate. I don't use the goals to beat myself up. I use them as guidelines to help me focus my learning. It is very encouraging to look back over the past few years and see what issues I have been working on and how I am progressing. Prior to setting yearly growth goals, I really could not remember what the issues had been two years before. Setting growth goals and writing them down has truly allowed me to focus in on the things that God is doing in my life.

Let me take it one step further and share with you how I work accountability into the mix. I have found that for me, unless I intentionally structure accountability into my life, it won't happen. Accountability for growth doesn't happen on its own. Here is what I do.

I write out my goals during the last part of December or the first part of January. I give a copy of them to my upward mentor. Presently, my father is operating as one of my upward mentors. I give him a copy of my goals and give him permission to ask me about how I am doing at any time. He usually asks me about something I am working on at least once a month. I give a copy to my wife. She really holds me accountable! We try to take two weekends a year (one in the spring and one in the fall) where we get out our goals and help each other assess how we are doing. We both have personal goals but also have goals that we work on as a couple. For example, last year we explored what "partnership in ministry" meant for us. We made some significant progress in understanding our individual giftedness and how we can work together. This year, one of our goals involves working out the implications of what we learned about ourselves last year.

In addition, I usually give a copy of my goals to a few of my peer mentors who have permission to ask "tough" questions at any time. I also share my goals with a number of my downward mentorees both to model growth goal setting and to let them hold me accountable.

I carry a copy of my goals with me in my calendar. I probably read through them about every two to three months. I try to evaluate and assess how I'm doing. Formally I evaluate how I'm doing during the weekend away with my wife.

At the end of the year, I reflect on my goals and this past year I wrote up an evaluation of how I did over the year. In past years, I have given a verbal report to my upward mentors and my wife. This year I tried writing the evaluation. I liked the process of writing out my evaluation. Plus, I now have a written evaluation which I file away.

By the way, I tend to be an optimistic goal setter. I have never been able to meet all of my goals...yet. I am getting better at setting more realistic goals each year. Last year, I estimated that I had done about 75% of what I had set out to do. I was really happy with that. I never seem to accomplish everything that I want to but I know one thing for sure, I am accomplishing way more that I would without the goals.

I'm sure for some of you this whole issue of accountability and goal setting seems rather foreign. I would encourage you to give it a try. Experiment with it and try to find something that works with you. Yearly goal setting is not something that works for everyone. There are other methods that work. I know of a couple of people who keep journals as their way of evaluating and reflecting on what they are learning. One of my mentorees attends a church where the members are encouraged to write a letter to God during a New Year's Eve service. In the letter, he/she is to tell God all the things that he/she would like Him to do in the next year. This isn't quite the same thing as setting growth goals but as I read his letter to God, that is exactly what he had done. He asked God to help him growth in certain areas.

The methods may differ but we all need to get some accountability for our growth. Without it, we will tend to plateau in our growth. Eventually we will decline. God believes in accountability. He is going to hold each one of us accountable for the way we have grown and the things that we have done.

A Final Exhortation

I wish that Paul and I could sit down with each one of you and encourage you personally. God loves you. He is with you. He wants you to grow and develop until you reach the maximum potential that He has for you. He is committed to the process of developing you. He is a loving God. He is a faithful God. He is merciful and compassionate. He is quick to respond in mercy.

I want to close with an image of God that Moses wrote about. It comes from Deuteronomy 32:10-11 He wrote, "In a desert land he found him, in a barren and howling waste. He shielded him and cared for him; he guarded him as the apple of his eye, **like an eagle that stirs up its nest and hovers over its young, that spreads it wings to catch them and carries them on its pinions.**" (NIV) Here is another translation. "He found them wandering through the desert, a desolate, wind-swept wilderness. He protected them and cared for them, as he would protect himself. **Like an eagle teaching its young to fly, catching them safely on its spreading wings, the Lord kept Israel from falling.**"(NEV)

Moses was singing a final song over the people of Israel. He was imparting his last words of leadership to the people. He uses the image of an eagle teaching its young to fly to talk about God. He had probably observed this image during one of his solitary sojourns up on the mountainside.

Try to capture the image that he used. Imagine looking up high on a cliff side. The parent eagle is hovering over the nest. In order to hover over the nest, the eagle has to beat its wings furiously. This is creating tremendous turbulence for the baby eagles. The baby eagles are pushed by the turbulence to the edge of the aerie. The turbulence of the parent's wings beating knocks the eaglet over the edge. The eaglet beats its young wings furiously trying to stay fixed on the edge of the nest. However, it can't stay and falls. It continues to beat its young wings but is not strong enough to fly. The eaglet falls and is headed for the rocks below. Before the eaglet hits the rocks, the parent eagle races down from above and spreads its wings underneath the baby eagle, catching and carrying the baby eagle to back to the aerie and safety.

This is the word picture that Moses uses to describe God and the way He has dealt with the people of Israel. The Lord protected and cared for them. Eventually they needed to grow and mature. God created turbulence around them. They had to learn to "fly".

Leadership development in God's kingdom involves the same dynamic. Have you ever encountered turbulence from God? Have you ever felt like you were pushed to the edge of the nest? Have you ever fallen? Have you tried to fly with all you had only to discover that you were still falling to a certain death? God wants you to learn to fly. He wants you to grow and mature. The process can be terrifying for some. However, don't forget the last piece of the image.

God swooping under you at the last moment to catch you on His strong back and carry you back to safety. Tomorrow the process will be repeated until you grow strong and learn to soar. Can you imagine how beautiful it is to watch a parent eagle with its young soaring on the updrafts?

Go deep with God. Let the crisis moments of life and ministry drive you deep into Him. Embrace the learning process. God will not disappoint you.

---

[1] J. Robert Clinton. Taken from research notes for a book yet to be published. The book is called: Focused Lives: Inspirational Life Changing Lessons From Eight Effective Christian Leaders Who Finished Well.

[2] A.W. Tozer, The Knowledge of the Holy. San Francisco: Harper and Row Publishers, 1961, p. 1.

References Cited

Anderson, Neil, *The Bondage Breaker.* Eugene, OR: Harvest House
Publishers, 1990.

Boice, James M., *Foundations of the Christian Faith.* Downers
Grove, IL: Intervarsity Press, 1986.

Bruce, A.B., *The Training of the Twelve.* Grand Rapids, MI: Kregel
Publications, 1971, 1988.

Clinton, J. Robert, *The Making of a Leader.* Colorado Springs,
CO: NavPress, 1988.

_____. *Leadership Emergence Theory.* Altadena, CA:
Barnabas Publishers, 1989.

_____. *"Social Base Processing".* Altadena, CA: Barnabas
Publishers, 1993.

Clinton, J. Robert and Richard W. Clinton, *The Mentor Handbook.*
Altadena, CA: Barnabas Publishers, 1992.

_____. *Developing Leadership Giftedness.* Altadena, CA:
Barnabas Publishers, 1993.

Clinton, J. Robert and Paul Stanley, *Connecting*. Colorado Springs: CO: NavPress, 1992.

Crabb, Larry, *Effective Biblical Counseling*. Grand Rapids, MI: Zondervan, 1977.

Davis, Ron Lee, *Mentoring: The Strategy of the Master*. Nashville, TN: Thomas Nelson Publishers, 1991.

Eastman, Dick, "*Challenge the World School of Prayer Manual*" Every Home For Christ International, 1991.

Edman, V. Raymond, *They Found the Secret*. Grand Rapids, MI: Zondervan, 1984.

Elwell, Walter A. *Encyclopedia of the Bible*. Grand Rapids, MI: Baker Book House, 1988.

_____. *Topical Analysis of the Bible*. Grand Rapids, MI: Baker Book House, 1991.

Engstrom, Ted and Norman B. Rohrer, *The Fine Art of Mentoring*. Brentwood, TN: Wolgemuth and Hyatt Publishers, 1989.

Foster, Richard, *Celebration of Discipline*. San Francisco: Harper and Row, 1978.

Grounds, Vernon, *Radical Commitment*. Portland, OR: Multnomah Press, 1984.

Hendricks, Howard, *Teaching to Change Lives*. Portland, OR: Multnomah Press and Walk Thru the Bible Ministries, 1987.

Lea, Larry, *The Hearing Word*. Altamonte Springs, FL: Creation House, 1988.

McGinnis, Alan Loy, *Bringing Out the Best in People*. Minneapolis, MN: Augsburg, 1985.

Meyers, F. B., *"Classic Portraits"* Series from Christian Literature Crusade
Abraham: The Obedience of Faith. Ft. Washington, PA: CLC, 1985.
Isreal:A Prince with God. Ft. Washington, PA: CLC, 1983.
Joseph: Beloved, Hated, Exalted. Ft. Washington, PA: CLC, no date.
Moses: The Servant of God. Ft. Washington, PA: CLC, 1984.
Joshua:And the Land of Promise. Ft. Washington, PA: CLC, 1977.
Samuel:The Prophet. Ft. Washington, PA: CLC, 1978.
David:Shepherd, Psalmist, King. Ft. Washington, PA: CLC, 1990.
Elijah: And the Secret of his Power. Ft. Washington, PA: CLC, 1978.
Jeremiah: Priest and Prophet. Ft. Washington, PA: CLC, 1988.
John:The Baptist. Ft. Washington, PA: CLC, 1988.
Peter: Fisherman, Disciple, Apostle. Ft. Washington, PA: CLC, 1978.
Paul:A Servant of Jesus Christ. Ft. Washington, PA: CLC, 1978.

Motyer, Alec *The Message of James*. Downers Grove, IL: Intervarsity Press, 1985.

Robertson, John, *The Timothy Principle*. Colorado Springs, CO: Navpress, 1986.

Roper, Dave, *The Law That Sets You Free*. Waco, TX: Word, 1977.

Ryrie, Charles, *So Great Salvation*. Wheaton, IL: Victor Books, 1989.

Sanders, J. Oswald, *Spiritual Leadership*. Chicago: Moody, 1989.

Stott, John, *Basic Christianity*. Downers Grove, IL: Intervarsity Press, 1971.

Tozer, A.W., *The Knowledge of the Holy.* San Francisco: Harper and Row Publishers, 1961

Vine, W.E., *Expository Dictionary of New Testament Words*. Old Tappan, NJ: Fleming H. Revell, 1966.

Virkler, Mark, *Dialogue With God*. Plainfield, NJ: Bridge Publishers, 1986.

Webster's Seventh New Collegiate Dictionary G & C Merriam Company, 1967.

Wimber, John and Kevin Springer, *Power Points*. San Francisco: HarperCollins, 1991.

Wrong, Dennis, Power: *Its Forms, Bases and Uses*. San Francisco: Harper and Row Publishers, 1979.

CPSIA information can be obtained at www.ICGtesting.com
Printed in the USA
BVOW02s0205220813

329272BV00001B/20/A

9 780974 181837